MW01258978

Get Over Yourself: How I Reversed My MS
By Kenneth F. Ciesla

No matter where you are on your journey, always know that your life is overwhelmingly blessed. Even if it doesn't seem that way. It is, and you are.

Disclaimer

This book is in no way meant to suggest, cure, or prevent any disease. Any information used should be done so with the guidance of a licensed medical doctor.

Table of Contents

Conclusion
page 132

Prologue

Shockingly enough, my first thought after being told I had symptoms suggestive of multiple sclerosis wasn't that I'd been handed a death sentence.

Sure, the initial *oh shit* shock wave went through me. But instead of that blank headspace someone who's just been handed the worst news of his life so often describes, I felt a sort of swelling inside of me I can only peg as a misplaced survival instinct. I'd just learned my mobility would continue getting worse. Eventually, I would have to say goodbye to the family I had just started.

Panic would have been rational.

Instead, I was filled with a sense of dire urgency and one frantic question: *How do I turn this around?*

I didn't know where that came from—I'm not one to carry a hero complex, and the whole defiance-of-the-medical-community-thing wasn't something I'd really ever subscribed to.
I get that denial is part of grief, but this wasn't quite that. I fully believed the test results; anyone would, after living through years of the symptoms I had. Denial's not the word. This was resistance, plain and simple. I believed the doctors—I just refused to believe the projected outcome.

I get that this isn't an entirely relatable reaction for a lot of people. That's why I'm sharing it. That resistance pushed me to seek answers that ultimately led me to reverse my diagnosis and its correlated symptoms that ailed me—all without a single prescribed drug, injection, hospital stay, or surgery.

I'm no doctor, and I can't promise that what I experienced would work for everyone. But perseverance over doubt and surrender, seeking answers where there were questions, and refusing to take something lying down are things we can all do physically and mentally. I'm sharing my story as a way to share hope. There is great power in being a seeker, finding peace within, and optimizing your own personal healthcare. Doing so reversed my symptoms. My hope is it can help you, too.

Part One: THE SYMPTOMS

When you sign on to a career as a plumber, you're agreeing to do any number of dirty jobs. Repairing clogged drains is a fraction of the gig; most of the time, you're soldering pipes together, working dusty construction sites without protective gear, digging, cutting concrete, laying water lines, you name it.

I was a career plumber. And a decade in, I'd worked my way up to a lot of repair jobs—more mainstream plumbing work, like repairing toilets and showers. You find yourself in all kinds of positions with this job—on your back in crawl spaces, navigating dusty basements, jammed up under tiny kitchen cabinets. One day, I reached up over my head to tighten a joint on some PVC pipe, and my arms stopped at about shoulder height.

I was in a cramped space and I'd been working like that for an hour or so, so I chalked it up to tight joints. I rolled my shoulders a couple of times, bent my head from side to side to stretch my neck, and reached up again.

Nothing.

There was a little bit of pain, like if you try to stretch a bit past your point of flexibility, but nothing too serious. It was simply that my range of motion ended right there, even with my shoulders. I quickly thought back through the last 24 hours, searching for an injury I'd forgotten. I couldn't think of anything strenuous I'd done the day before, or out of the ordinary that morning. Still, raising my arms was hopeless.

It reminded me of a few times as a teenager when a particular limb wouldn't work. Nothing serious, more like a sense of numbness or limited mobility for a few seconds at a time and then everything righted itself and I'd forget about it. Funny that I suddenly recalled that, like the opposite of a muscle memory: a failed-muscle memory.

I told the guys I was working with, who were skeptical of my injury. But for the next month, I could only raise my forearms while my elbows hung at my sides. I did my best to find workarounds, but one day my boss sent me out to do a water heater and I had to tell him I couldn't. At that point, this one physical limitation was wreaking havoc on all kinds of daily tasks, from driving to working under kitchen sinks.

When my co-workers started to complain and I realized my arms weren't getting any better, I made an appointment to see the doctor. And when he realized this was no sore muscle, he ordered an MRI.

The MRI showed nothing, so he made an educated guess that it was probably bursitis, a painful condition caused by inflammation in the small, fluid-filled sacs that cushion your bones, tendons and muscles near your joints. The most common locations for BURSITIS are in the shoulders, elbows and hips.

I was sent home with a giant rubber band to connect to a doorknob and instructed to do uncomfortable arm exercises to strengthen my muscles. I did the exercises, and the symptoms did go away. But it wasn't gradual—they were just there one day, gone the next. I was thrilled to be healed and quickly forgot about the whole ordeal.

Five years passed. I started my own plumbing business, got married, and had a newborn baby girl.

One day while driving in my work van, I felt a strange pressure on the top of my head. It was only for a split second, so I ignored it. But over the next month, those sensations came more frequently, and with increasing severity. So, I started clocking time between sensations. In a typical day, they were coming on every 0 to 15 minutes, and lasting anywhere from 30 seconds to a minute. The pressure bent me over as if someone was sitting on my back. There wasn't any pain, but the pressure was horribly uncomfortable and left me dizzy. It also messed with my speech: If I didn't focus with all my power on my speech, it slurred like I was drunk.

Meeting with prospective clients for my plumbing business was becoming almost impossible. One day, I met a potential client at a coffee shop to discuss a new project. I could hardly look at them, let alone keep my speech on point. The pressure on my head was totally distracting. I barely made it through the meeting, trying desperately to hide my symptoms.

Hiding the symptoms while working was also proving particularly trying.

I'd begun installing solar hot water systems despite never feeling comfortable climbing ladders and working on steep rooftops. I've always had a fear of heights, but it hadn't made me dizzy. Then, suddenly, being high up in the air gave me terrible vertigo. The symptom became too much to handle. I didn't want to fall and be a liability. I stopped working on rooftops. The symptoms were a valid reason for me to stay on the ground.

I tried to convince myself that I could manage what was happening to me, so I compare it to something familiar: partying. When I was younger, I'd stumbled and slurred my speech from being completely inebriated. I utilized the same tools for covering up this mysterious impairment. But despite those efforts, nothing was allowing me to function at normal velocity.

Partying and experimentation years earlier had affected my memory, but now it was more fleeting every day. I forgot to pay bills. Simple tasks were falling by the wayside. I was in a constant state of brain fog.

For the most part, I kept quiet about what I was going through. I didn't want to worry anyone. But as basic activities became impossible in the face of my worsening symptoms, my ability to hide them became laborious. Six months in, I scheduled another doctor's appointment.

Part Two: THE DIAGNOSIS

"I think I might have vertigo."

Understatement of the year.

I sat on the exam table at my local urgent care clinic, rubbing my palms together and willing them to stop sweating. I looked past the doctor at a poster on the back of the door showing illustrations of flu symptoms. "Should I go to an eye doctor? Or do you think maybe an ear, nose and throat doctor?" I was babbling now, not waiting for an answer. "Or a neurologist?"

The last word came out dry from my throat. I swallowed.

Seeing a neurologist meant something was wrong deep inside of me. My muscles. My nerves. My brain. I thought of my daughter; only a few months old. My wife, who thought I was taking a lunch break from work with the guys.

Please, anything but a neurologist.

My "vertigo" wasn't a passing symptom. What started as light-headedness when I stood up had evolved into constant dizziness, obvious cognitive decline, and a lack of coordination that made even brushing my teeth a feat of sheer will. I told myself persistent migraines were to blame for the steep decline in my plumbing career. I told my wife I was overtired. The few friends I confided in assured me it was nothing.

I knew it was denial. No plumber worth his salt can't tighten a simple drain fitting.

Our egos are good at tapping into survival instincts. We create illusions so we can face the unbearable.

But even egos have a breaking point.

The doctor tested my reflexes and had me stand on one foot with my arms out. She told me to shut my eyes and touch my nose as if I'd been pulled over for drunk driving. And without skipping a beat, she told me to make an appointment with a neurologist.

For two more weeks, I kept up the charade at home and at work with my symptoms in a strange, stoic holding pattern I was fighting to hide. Then I was off to another waiting room in another New Jersey doctor's office, having told yet another lie to my wife about where I was.

At 32, I was the youngest person in there. I eyed elderly patients suffering from dementia and other conditions much, much worse. Thirty minutes went by with me agonizing over whether I had a brain tumor or a severe case of hypochondria.

Then, while seated on yet another, increasingly familiar exam table, I repeated all my symptoms to the neurologist. The clamminess I'd grown used to crept along my hands and neck.

He listened intently, jotting down notes. "We're going to begin with some physical tests," he said, and had me walk back and forth on a straight line he laid out on the floor with masking tape. My walk was off. I knew it but didn't want to show him. I overcompensated, as I'd learn to do in the last few months, trying to hide the subtle stumbles by favoring my left side and extending my fingers for balance.

Those tests were followed by muscle-reflex tests on my hands, arms and legs. The doctor told me he couldn't see any obvious issues but wanted an MRI. Another appointment. More waiting.

The neurologist went over the MRI's findings with me a week later. Conducted without contrast dye, the test had shown very little. Here's the full rundown, verbatim, in classic doctoral gibberish:

"The ventricles and sulci are normal for the patient's age. There are extensive areas of hyper-intensity in the periventricular white matter, the frontal, parietal, and temporal lobes. Subcortical lesions are noted in the frontal lobes bilaterally and in the left parietal vertex. There is a lesion in the left cerebellar vermis. Supplemental high-resolution sagittal flair sequences disclose a perivenular disposition of lesions in the septal callosal interface. There are no other abnormal areas of parenchymal signal intensity. Gradient echo images disclose no evidence of current or previous hemorrhage. There are no areas of restricted aqueous diffusion on DWI. There are no masses or extra-axial collections. The visualized paranasal sinuses and mastoid processes are clear.

Impression: areas hyper-intensity in the periventricular white matter of the frontal, parietal, and temporal lobes. There are subcortical areas of hyper-intensity in the frontal lobes and left parietal lobe vertex. There is a focal lesion in the left cerebellar hemisphere. Supplemental high-resolution sagittal flair sequences disclose a perivenular disposition of lesions in the septal callosal interface. The appearance is most consistent with demyelinating disease."

In other words, the test was inconclusive. My doctor ordered another MRI, this time with contrast— meaning I'd be shot up with a gadolinium-rich dye that would light my bloodstream like lightning to enhance the imaging.

Two MRIs, 14 days apart.

The second report changed everything:

"The ventricles, sulci and basal cisterns are normal in size and configuration. There is no extra-axial collection, mass effect or midline shift. There are multiple foci of hyper-intensity in the periventricular, deep and subcortical white matter bilaterally. None of the lesions are enhancing. The lesions in the cerebellar vermis adjacent to the fourth ventricle appear less conspicuous than on the prior study. Otherwise, the lesions are unchanged. No evidence of recent infarct on diffusion images. There is no abnormal enhancement of the brain or meninges. Gradient echo demonstrates no evidence of hemorrhage. The major intracranial flow voids are preserved. Thin section images demonstrate no abnormal signal, enhancement, or evidence of mass effect within the cerebellopontine angles, internal auditory canals or inner ears. There is no evidence of thickening or modularity of the 7th and 8th nerves. Fluid-filled structures of the inner ears demonstrate normal configuration. The mastoid air cells clear. The paranasal sinuses are clear. The orbits are unremarkable.

Impression: Numerous non-enhancing white matter lesions are described. This is suggestive of multiple sclerosis and clinical correlation and follow-up is recommended. Evaluation of IACs is unremarkable.

One line jumped out at me: "Suggestive of multiple sclerosis." The dizziness was overwhelming now. I could barely hear the doctor talking.

"Do you know what a brain lesion is?" he asked.

"No."

"A lesion is another word for a scar. If I scratch you on the arm and you develop a scar, you know how you got that scar. We do not know how, or why, you have scars on your brain."

Stunned silence.

"We have one more test I'd like to perform, to rule out multiple sclerosis."

"What kind of test?" I asked, my brain floating out above my body. Outer space and nowhere at all. I dug my left index finger into my palm, focusing on the phrase "to rule out" more than the diagnosis.

"You're going to need a spinal tap."

I don't remember making the appointment for the spinal tap, leaving the neurologist's office, or going home. I was in my body but not, terrified but too terrified to feel it. The not-knowing and growing anticipation, combined with my already failing coordination and diminishing sense of control over my own limbs and brain, had peaked.

At the neurologist's office a few days later, we found out that the test was proof positive: I was exhibiting clear symptoms of one fatal diagnosis: multiple sclerosis. The official report read, verbatim:

The patient's CSF contained four well-defined gamma restriction bands that are not present in the patient's corresponding serum sample. These bands indicate an abnormal synthesis of gamma globulins in the central nervous system. This finding is supportive evidence of multiple sclerosis but should be interpreted in conjunction with all clinical and laboratory data pertaining to this patient.

I walked up the front steps of my own house that day, holding onto the railing and feeling it for the first time.

My wife knew something was wrong—had known something was wrong, no matter how well I tried to hide my symptoms from her. Her tears started coming before I'd gotten through the first sentence: a release that came from the validation of her worst fears.

Reassuring her was useless. My insistence that things would be fine was a transparent lie, and she called me out on it. "What are we going to do?" she cried, at once angry at me for trying to hide my symptoms for so long, furious at herself for going along with my denial, and in anguish over what I was going through. I could see her own egoic struggle as she transitioned from worry for our baby, sorrow for herself, and compassion for me.

But I meant it—I was certain I could be OK. There had to be a way to make things right.

We talked for hours, making plans for how to tell our family and closest friends, and going over logistics for every possible scenario. We got angry. We cried. And climbing out from the shadows left me oddly invigorated.

A looming spinal tap is enough to scare anyone, I don't care who you are. In the days leading up to the procedure, all you can think of is a giant, hollow needle driving into your back. As someone who used to faint anytime my blood was drawn, this imaging was enough to put me over the edge I was already barely hanging onto.

A nurse came with a long needle that looked like something out of a torture chamber. Luckily for me, everything was happening out of my range of site. Once the local anesthetic was doing its work, I didn't have any pain at all. To my absolute relief and delight, I only felt pressure, like someone pushing on my back.

I celebrated afterward by going for ice cream with my wife and friends. It was like I'd just overcome something—not only just begun.

The doctor prescribed a drug called Avonex injection #12 vial and had me visit an MS center in northern New Jersey so I could learn how to administer the drug to myself. That's it: there was no cure for MS, he said; just inject these drugs and learn to manage.

I never injected the Avonex, even as new symptoms developed; like numbness along my right cheek and the side of my neck. I wasn't going to just roll over for the diagnosis.

But all around me, the MS classification was disrupting everything—and well beyond my symptoms.

The most stunning life change when you have an illness isn't the never-ending stream of doctors' appointments or lab tests. It's not the incessant worrying about the future, either. The biggest change comes in how differently the people you know and love act. That diagnosis becomes larger than you. It isn't simply one piece of your life right now; it becomes something that takes on a life of its own. It defines you, becomes the primary topic of conversation, and makes everyone around you nervous.

"How are you today?" takes on whole new meaning. Your friends and family all want updates from the doctor. When people aren't talking about your illness, they're tiptoeing around you. The pity is overwhelming.

I got the feeling that some people were acting like I was going to die. I knew better, as crazy as that sounds. I didn't want to worry anyone, but I didn't want to hear, "Why didn't you tell me?" either. It was easier to be out in the open now.

I asked the neurologist if there were any natural alternatives to the injections.

"I'm not trained for vitamins," he said.

But I wasn't trained for the side effects of heavy-duty medications. I wasn't prepared to languish. And I wasn't about to just roll over and do as I was told. There had been no discussion of what might be causing these MS-like symptoms, and no talk of an actual cure.

So, I set out to find the answers myself.

Part Three: FINDING THE ROOT CAUSES

Demyelinating diseases are a classification of nervous-system diseases that involves damage caused to the myelin sheath of neurons. Multiple sclerosis, or MS, is the most common demyelinating disease.

The myelin sheath is a protective covering that surrounds nerves in your brain and spinal cord. When the myelin is damaged, nerve impulses slow or even stop, causing neurological problems that can run the gamut from coordination problems to paralysis. When you have MS, your immune system mistakenly attacks the myelin sheath, or the cells that produce and maintain the myelin. This causes inflammation and injury to the sheath, and ultimately to the nerves it surrounds. The result can be multiple areas of scarring (sclerosis), which can eventually slow or block nerve signals that control muscle coordination, strength, sensation, and vision.

MS is all about inflammation—and we can all relate to those things that cause inflammation, whether physical or mental. Inflammation can be a shitty attitude as much as it can be a swollen joint. Bad coping mechanisms are inflammatory. Processed foods are inflammatory. There are many levels, and many ways, of inflammation.

To fight these symptoms, I would have to fight that whatever was causing the inflammation. And to do that, I had to first consider what in my life could be a contributing factor.

Airborne carcinogens

I tried my first cigarette when I was 14 years old. By the time I was 16, I was a regular smoker. In high school, it was totally normal for students to smoke on school property. Sometimes they did it right in front of the school's entrance alongside teachers.

I stopped smoking two years prior to getting diagnosed.

Heavy metal toxicity
Heavy metal toxicity is another cause of inflammation in the body. People are exposed to these poisons every day: from mercury amalgam tooth fillings to certain brands of make-up. But for me, there were three very direct connections to toxic metals.

I went to a vocational high school for plumbing. It was there I was first exposed to melting lead. With good intention, the instructor wanted to teach us how things had been done by generations past. We would melt the lead outside in the summertime, because the burner would get too hot and we would sweat too much working with it indoors. But in the winter, we always melted the lead in a big pot inside. It helped to warm up the shop on really cold days. Little did any of us understand the potential consequences of this.

You know the smoke that appears when you overheat cooking oil in a skillet? That smoke is essentially a vapor you can see. The same thing happens to heavy metals when they melt. One difference, however, is that you cannot see heavy metal vapors. Heavy metals are a known neurotoxin, and when you melt any heavy metal, unless it is isolated you are breathing in those toxic vapors and your brain is getting damaged. We all stood in front of the burner with molten lead in that shop room. We all had brain cells damaged from exposure.

Plumbers are exposed to a myriad of toxins, including toxic dust at job sites from plaster and concrete, glues and primers for joining waste and water systems, and of course, lead. Two more toxins are byproducts of a process called "sweating the joint," or "fitting." To sweat a joint, a small amount of a chemical called flux is brushed around the end of a copper tube and fitting. The two pieces are pushed together and the joint is heated at high temperatures. The flux begins to melt, which helps to clean the joint. The flux is also the agent that pulls the melted solder (tin) into the joint. This process exposes you to two toxic vapors: smoke from the flux, and vapor from the melted tin (solder).

Street drugs
After high school, I experimented with LSD in pill, paper, and straight liquid form. I also experimented with magic mushrooms and cocaine (though I'd hardly call one five-day banger "experimentation"). There was also a period of time when some friends and I messed around inhaling nitrous gas from a balloon, or from a friend's father's tank in his dental office. I also tried MDMA, or ecstasy, out at some clubs.

I was partying too much and doing major damage to my body and nervous system. I don't mess with that stuff anymore.

Emotional components
Stress is among the most inflammatory agents our bodies have to contend with. Not keeping our emotions in check can cause extensive physical damage.

MS is a disease rooted in anger. Experiencing strong negative emotions and traumas floods the body with destructive hormones and chemicals, weakening the immune system or causing it to act in inflammatory ways. When most people get sick, they look to western medicine or diet for the answers without also addressing the emotional components that can make us the sickest. Cultivating peace in your heart is the antithesis.

Part Four: ACCEPTING THE REALITIES OF CAUSE-AND-EFFECT

I've been in the plumbing trade for 25 years now, and many of my colleagues in the industry cast doubt on my medical history. "I've been pouring lead joints for years," they'll say, "how come *I* don't have multiple sclerosis?"

That's a fair question. Based on what I've learned through my own research, it occurs to me that disease is highly personalized.

How can one person do something destructive to their body every day and experience symptoms in one part of the body, yet another person can be just as self-destructive and have symptoms manifest elsewhere? The body responds to genetic predisposition combined with environmental conditions, thus effecting gene expression and expressing as symptoms.

Consider two people with arthritis. One has it in his arm, the other in her leg. The person with symptoms in his arm does something to heal his arthritis. Since arthritis is arthritis no matter where you have it, it would be silly for the person with arthritis in her leg not to try what he did for his arm. Treatment for arthritis in the arm can have the same effect on another person in her leg because arthritis is arthritis. The only difference is where it happens in the body. Autoimmune disease is this way.

What that formula is and what the results are may differ in everyone, but we all know that our bodies respond to family history along with our own habits and behaviors. The gene exists, and our choices determine if and how they express themselves. Eating a diet high in unhealthy fats like deep fried foods can produce pancreatitis for one and heart disease for another. This is because parts of our bodies have a genetic predisposition to be weak. The weakest link in the chain always breaks first. Certain weaknesses eventually present in response to one factor or another. It's a matter of when, and where on the body, from person to person. The fact that I was diagnosed with MS symptoms at 32 doesn't mean you will have the same illness from the same inflammatory sources.

That said, you might develop something else as an older person from the same type of toxic overload.

In my family, illness seems to manifest in our brains. My Grandma had bipolar disorder, and a number of other family members have faced a myriad of mental health issues. For whatever reason, my family's brains seem to be the organ manifesting the most health issues in our family.

To have my immune system work more effectively, I had to give it a rest. That meant no longer doing things that gave my immune system a reason to activate—or, in regard to MS—*hyperactivate*.

Part Five: CHOOSING A PATH

How will I conquer this? Can I conquer this? What should I do? Do I take the drugs? Do I try something different? To pick a path forward, I had to first consider each of my options.

Conventional
Based on what I read and my neurologist explained, conventional medicine looks at MS as something that happens to you. It's a random attack perpetrated by the immune system on the protective covering of your nerves and brain, creating scars. The medical community doesn't know why it happens, though speculation says the reason an autoimmune disease comes about in the first place is due to an inflammatory response caused by your immune system attacking the body.

Bodies can only tolerate so much inflammation before they reach their tipping points, which are manifested as symptoms. Those symptoms appear where the physical damage is occurring; which is why they can vary so wildly from one person to the next. Lesions in the brain can form in any variety and combination.

A board-certified medical professional broke MS down for me like this: "Your immune system has changed its mind, and now wants to hurt you instead of protect you." Western medicine as a whole operates under the notion that there is no cure for MS. If you follow this line of thinking, it makes sense that pharmaceuticals would be used to manage symptoms. At the end of the day, you are nothing more than a victim of a malfunction from your own body.

Have a symptom? There's a pill for that.

The prevailing approach for many as-yet understood diseases is, simply, symptom management and preparation for the worst.

But what if you don't want to simply manage symptoms? What if you want to eliminate the possibility of symptoms coming back for good without a dependency on pharmaceuticals? If you want to follow the second path, you have to consider the source of your illness and fight that. And that's where holistic medicine comes in.

Holistic

Holistic medicine does not subscribe to conventional medicine's belief that disease is the body behaving inappropriately. Instead, holistic medicine operates under the guise that the body is acting appropriately to remove something that doesn't belong—even if it means going through healthy tissue to eliminate the toxins and stop the inflammation.

In this way of thinking, the disease of the categorized symptoms are real. However, the disease itself may not exist; only emotional or physical imbalances that manifest in symptoms. Holistic medicine makes no promises but does offer hope. The approach is simple: Remove any harmful heavy metals, viruses or toxins in the body that can cause inflammation. Avoid the foods and environments that contribute to inflammation. You help yourself when you remove the toxins, so your body can focus on repair and healing.

I am not a medical professional; but as a consumer, it made sense to me to integrate conventional and holistic medicinal approaches. Depending on what ailments you are facing, traditional medicine may be necessary. But in addition, we do ourselves a grave disservice if we ignore all the natural ways we can help and heal our bodies' systems. As far as I know, a person has never died from eating a healthy diet or making healthy lifestyle changes.

Conventional medicine dictates that the inflammation from MS is caused by the immune system arbitrarily attacking the body; while holistic medicine believes the inflammation comes from a toxic agent that causes the immune system to hyperactivate and attempt to remove the toxin.

My western-practicing doctor told me there was no cure for what ailed me; and advised pharmaceuticals to help ease my discomfort. I did not blame him for his perspective because I understand he was only implementing the information he's been trained to use. But when I looked past that option and into the alternative health field, I discovered a spectrum of other options available to me that had the potential to not only curb my symptoms but heal me completely.

Looking back now, I'm grateful for the diagnosis I got. Without it, I wouldn't be where I am now. The illness forced me to connect the dots between my lifestyle and overall wellness. Everything in my life became about self-discovery. Who am I? What am I made of? Who has the power—me or the disease?

Part Six: WALKING THE PATH

A friend that taught me so many lessons in business named Bob Kane once told me, "the amount of success we can achieve is in direct proportion to our ability and willingness to ask questions."

I spoke earlier about influential health factors I was exposed to throughout my life: family genetics, workplace safety hazards, and personal choices and lifestyle patterns. If the MS symptoms I experienced were actually a genetically weakened response to exposure to harmful chemicals and heavy metals, then I needed to make a conscious effort to expose myself to things that may offer a more positive reaction.

Similarly, if any of my symptoms could be traced back to negative behaviors, thought patterns or dysfunctions, then I needed to change my way of thinking and being to something in harmony and positive. Bottom line? If we do what we've always done, then we'll get what we've always gotten.

My first call was to a Reiki master.

Reiki is the practice of healing a person's body through energy points, or chakras. The term "Reiki" comes from two Japanese words: Rei, or higher power; and Ki, which means life force energy. Chakras are points of energy in various spots of the body that allow for the flow of energy. Chakras can become blocked by an emotional or physical trauma, conflict, or physical ailment. When a blockage happens, there is a physical disruption of energy flow throughout the body. These blockages can manifest physically as disease, chronic aches, and pains, or mentally as high-stress, anxiety and confusion.

A Reiki practitioner uses various techniques to open the energy channels or chakras. One is a "laying of the hands" process in which the master puts his or her hands near the blocked chakra in order to transfer life force energy into the subject to clear the blockage. Reiki masters can also send Reiki with their thoughts, or work in a group with fellow Reiki masters.

The Reiki master I called was Fotini Papasavvas, a friend of my wife's who had helped her years before with a thyroid issue that doctors wanted to operate on. Instead of scheduling surgery, my wife scheduled a visit with Fotini. The Reiki master told my wife that thyroid problems can relate back to feelings of dissatisfaction or humiliation; and explained that the language we speak to ourselves can cause a chakra to close. They had two sessions together before my wife went back to her doctor for a follow-up.

He checked her thyroid and found entirely different results. There was no longer any reason to operate. My wife never had an issue with her thyroid again.

When I met with Fotini, she said I had holes inside my head—not dissimilar from her experience with other clients who had been through issues with hard drugs. I never considered myself a drug addict, because I could stop on my own without any intervention. But addict or not, I knew that in my day I had done more than my share of damage.

Fotini recommended I get a hair analysis done for heavy metals. These tests can review much older information than a blood or urine test, since the minerals that were in your hair when it was formed don't change over time.

I did as the Reiki master instructed and discovered that my tin and copper levels were off the charts. Here's the full rundown of the results:

Heavy Metal	Reference Range	My Level
Antimony	0.016	0.193

Arsenic	0.080	0.098
Cadmium	0.022	0.564
Lead	0.700	54.806
Tin	0.149	1.550
Copper	Nutrient Level 8-136	138

Looking over these numbers, I thought back to all those classes in high school when I would pour lead joints and solder copper and tin without protective masks… and all the years since. My body was toxic. I held onto this information until I knew what to do with it.

I went back to Fotini for more answers, only to discover she was leaving for Greece. She gave me a gift before she left: She attuned me to receive Reiki energy. An attunement is when a Reiki master imparts upon a student the ability to become a conduit of universal energy themselves for the purpose of healing. An attunement is achieved during an enhanced Reiki session that also employs a set of hand symbols.

There are three levels to Reiki on the way to mastership. In Reiki I, you have enough energy to light a stadium. Reiki II allows you to light up a continent. And Reiki III lets you light up the planet. A Reiki master can light the universe. Without teaching me any technique, Fotini attuned me to Reiki energy that would be constantly available for me to access. This was the first of many gifts I would get from the people who wanted to help me. Having this gift amplified the effect of everything else to come. Fotini eventually attuned my daughter, as well.

I joke sometimes, saying she made us all strong with the force.

My increasingly worried wife said I needed to email health advocate, talk show host, and author Gary Null, whose radio program she listened to frequently. On that broadcast, Null often said he does not turn down an opportunity to help a person and is always happy to give out protocols to those in need who ask for them.

Gary Null is a big name in the holistic movement. He rose to fame in the 1970s with his first book, *The Complete Guide to Health and Nutrition*, and a series of articles he co-authored for *Penthouse* called "The Politics of Cancer." He's known for being at odds with mainstream medicine, with some of his claims attacked by the medical community for allegedly being inconsistent with other published research and known data.

Personally, I've found a lot of inspiration in what Gary has to say. With each of his lectures I attend, I'm more convinced by how much power each of us has to determine our own wellness. This is less about specific medical claims he's made and more about the ability we all have to be in the moment and to treat the here and now as a chance to learn something, have fun, and move toward the light. I am endlessly grateful to Gary for these lessons.

When I emailed him out of the blue, I asked for an all-natural protocol for MS. Gary replied two days later, with an email that did nothing more than recommend three of his books: *Mind Power*, *Power Aging*, and *The Complete Encyclopedia of Natural Healing*. At the end of the email, he said when I was done with those books I should call holistic neurologist and homeopath Dr. Martin Feldman, who co-authored a book with Gary called *Death by Medicine.*

My heart sank. I thought his reply would include a straightforward plan of taking this herb or that supplement. Was this guy offering me a path, or shamelessly peddling his own works? Nevertheless, I got the books and dutifully read them cover to cover. And I was completely blown away.

Gary Null's books were like gold to me. The information and clarity he shares is valuable even if you're generally in good health. The education on the human body alone changed my entire way of looking at medicine and wellness. With the reading portion of my assignment over, I called up Dr. Feldman's office for an appointment.

A holistic neurologist's office is a bit different from a traditional doctor's office. The environment and vibe are all high-energy and bright: bright yellow walls, white floors and modern New York City fashion. Receptionists were all very nice but direct in an "OK, what are you here for?" kind of a way.

After sitting with Dr. Feldman and explaining my symptoms and diagnosis, he taught me about applied kinesiology.

Applied kinesiology is a method by which a practitioner detects various imbalances in the body, and allergies in the body's meridian system. The meridian system is a series of energy points all over the body, each of which is associated to an organ or body part. A practitioner with full understanding of applied kinesiology can read your body by checking muscle weakness or strength.

Dr. Feldman prescribed some supplements and told me to start on chelation therapy, the administration of chelating agents to remove heavy metals from the body. I did a lot of searching on the internet for a doctor who performed this (not an easy task), and miraculously found a doctor five minutes from home. His name was Richard Menashe. But before making an appointment, I consulted Dr. Feldman, to discuss. He had me come back in for a kinesiology appointment to test my metal toxicity.

Kinesiology, or biomechanics, is the study of body movement. Applied kinesiology is a form of muscle-strength testing based on the belief that specific muscles correlate with various organs and glans. Muscle weakness can therefore signify organ dysfunction related to things like chemical imbalances, nerve damage, food sensitivities, organ issues, and—in my case—metal toxicity. Dr. Feldman put various metals in my hand and then pressed on my muscles to see which affected my resistance strength.

My muscles couldn't stand any of them.

Dr. Feldman also gave me some guidance for my consult with Dr. Menashe, and said to keep him posted on my progress.

On my way home that day, it occurred to me to look for Gary Null's vitamin closet at his east side location in New York City, as it wasn't too far from Dr. Feldman's office. When I found the place, there was a short, hunched-over guy who introduced himself as Harry standing out front. Harry couldn't have been more than 5'4", with curly salt-and-pepper hair, dark eyebrows and shorts. He was standing outside waiting for a delivery. Turns out, he worked at the vitamin closet. We talked for the next 45 minutes, then wandered upstairs to check out the products.

As I scanned the floor-to-ceiling shelves brimming with posters of Gary's various books and documentaries, I told Harry about my MS symptoms. He asked me if I was in the new support group that was about to begin, explaining that Gary had recently formed a health support group for people with brain diseases like Parkinson's, MS and Alzheimer's. He figured I would take part in it, so he gave me the group discount in advance.

To join the group, Gary's rule was that you needed an actual diagnosis from a conventional doctor as proof. I quickly mailed all my information in, buzzing with the sense that big changes were coming. I passed time as I awaited a reply by working as I had before, continuing my lifestyle with little change, and scheduling an appointment with Richard Menashe for chelation therapy.

Dr. Menashe gave me an education on chelation therapy and what it can do. Chelating agents like EDTA and DMPS mind themselves to the heavy metals so the body can easily eliminate them. But before we started any treatment, he ordered a urine toxic metals test from Doctors Data, Inc.

My hair analysis had not shown any elevated mercury levels, but this urine toxic metals test showed elevated heavy metal levels for mercury and lead. Each has two sets of reference ranges, referred to on the report as "creat reference." Here are those results:

The creat reference range for mercury is 3, my level was 7.2.
The reference range for lead is 5, my level was 6.6.
The reference range for mercury is 5, my level was 11.
The reference for lead is 6, my level was 10.

Later, I received an email from Gary Null saying I had been accepted into his health support group. I was thrilled by the news—in no small part because at this point, despite my best efforts and a significant amount of education, my symptoms had not changed.

Part Seven: FINDING (AND ACCEPTING) SUPPORT

My personal and professional lives were as stressful as ever.

On a business level, I was in the third year of running my own plumbing company. It had been easy in the beginning, evening though like many contractors I'd started with very little money. Work was steady enough to compensate for that and I was one of those guys who enjoyed jumping into the water feet-first and without a single swim lesson.

Sink or swim.

I wasn't afraid because I had seen many do it successfully. I took my time with my clients and made their satisfaction my number-one priority. If I made a mistake, I'd own up to it and rectify the issue immediately. Eventually, against my wife's advice, I took out a loan to buy tools, stock the van, and get the van painted and lettered. She warned that I should wait until I was more established. She had my best interests at heart. But like those who join the dark side of the force, I chose the quick and easy path.

Then business slowed down. In addition, the countrywide financial crash that occurred that year didn't help. But my illness made it so much worse.

My short-term memory loss was wreaking havoc on my professional life; from unpaid bills to forgotten conversations. My whole existence was happening through a thick brain fog. Even my cognition felt like it was on a slippery slope.

Each poor choice only added to the storm. Although jobs were coming in and the phone was ringing, money would leave one hand shortly after the other received it. My poor spending habits and lack of financial and emotional discipline made it impossible to save for a rainy day. Unbeknownst to me, that rainy day was right around the bend. I was like the Titanic. I allowed my ego to delude me in a way that I didn't see the iceberg right in front of me. That "iceberg" was the year 2008; when then local economy stopped dead and I became more and more like a cat chasing his tail. The bills were paid, but always late.

All of this did not bode well for a young family just starting out. The best part of that year was the birth of my daughter. As difficult as things got, she was always the one that kept my world bright and shiny. As much shame that I had over my MS symptoms, I was even more embarrassed by my struggles to financially support my wife and child. I kept a front about my symptoms with people. I covered up the anxiety I felt about my fleeting ability to be a provider. My wife, who like many people entered a relationship with certain ideals and expectations for their future, was watching her sense of security shatter.

"Is everything OK?" she would ask me.

"Absolutely," I'd always reply. This answer was, of course, an absolute lie that only served my own, short-sighted desire for peace.

Avoid, avoid, avoid was my modus operandi.

When the phone stopped ringing, some of the bills stopped being paid. I got a call one day while on the job site: my wife.

"Ken! Why is the water shut off to our house?!"

I'd forgotten about the water bill. Apart from my stress level and lack of funds, my MS symptoms had severely affected my memory. Sometimes things simply didn't get paid.

Everyone has innate skills and abilities. My wife's was to save as much money as she could. My special skill was to spend (sometimes frivolously), the more the better. Like many relationships, our different habits surrounding money were huge points of contention. I knew I had to learn as much as possible about managing money. But more than that, I wanted to keep my family together. We worked around my weakness by ensuring all the money I earned would be spoken for by the time payday came around.

That plan didn't make me accountable, though. And eventually my avoidance and her frustration came to a head.

Not being able to fulfill the tribal instinct to provide for my wife and six-month-old badly bruised my confidence and self-esteem. But if things looked bad then, they were about to get worse.

One month, our family pastor paid the mortgage for us. That was the final straw. I filed for bankruptcy. My wife had no clue—I was too nervous to tell her. I just thought things would turn around. Plus, I was shit-scared of the conflict. Not good timing when trying to battle MS and the expenses that came with that. I turned to my spiritual healers for advice and help. Multiple visits to our Reiki healer, Fotini, and our acupuncturist, Bobby Aduna, brought only temporarily senses of wellness. We were still fighting. We were still spending above our means. And worst of all, I was still taking my wife and her contributions for granted.

When my wife learned about me filing for bankruptcy (no lie stays hidden forever), her confidence in me severed once and for all. My self-defeating behaviors had brought us to the brink. I was a dying husband, sick with a chronic illness that hindered my ability to support our young family. But worse than that, I had been spending more effort avoiding and lying than working to turn things around.

Even after this, we continued to try. My wife and I tackled the finances by spending even more money on seminars and classes to learn about real estate investing and different methods of money management. We promised to keep fighting, even as that bright future we battled for grew darker.

The first day I went to the support group, I was filled with anticipation over what to expect. Fortunately, my wife went along. She helped me climb the stairs and kept me from falling while I walked.

The space was mobbed with people, only adding to my anxiety. At the front of the room, cameras were set up to record our names and illnesses, which I had no idea would be happening. Sweat broke out over my entire body. The flight reflex was kicking in. But of course, I had signed whatever papers I needed to sign granting permission. Plus, I wasn't nimble enough to get up and run.

Sharing my illness, insecurities and truths in front of a huge crowd—and cameras—felt like submitting as weak. I didn't want to be seen as victim, least of all by myself. But lo and behold, we were asked to go around the room and list our symptoms.

I looked out into the crowd and spotted Dr. Feldman and of course Gary Null. I felt some of the awkwardness dissipate. And as I listened to people listing the same symptoms I was experiencing, I didn't feel like a victim—I felt like a sick person looking for answers.

Still, when my turn came I was shaking from the nerves and had sweat pooling everywhere.

After explaining our symptoms, we were instructed to immediately stop all consumption of meat, wheat, dairy and sugar; as many brain disorders are triggered by cerebral allergens. We were put on a 100-percent, allergy-free program. I had started the gradual transition to eating all-organic food, but truth be told I was frequently succumbing to temptation and consuming pork rinds, fast-food burgers, pizza, pretzel-covered hot dogs, and deep-fried everything.

It takes six months to one year to detoxify from those products, mainly because it took your entire life to get to this point. The detox diet cleanses all cells. To mitigate the effects of such a jolting transition, we were told to take many supplements to enhance our immune systems.

Then Dr. Feldman spoke about reducing allergy/allergens. Here are the notes I took:
- Allergy testing and allergy history.
- Journaling for allergies. Record what you ate and what kind of environment you were in. Must include time of day and time of year.
- Allergy-proof your home using a HEPA purifier. Put a purifier in bedroom and living room.
- Test for mold in home and office. Some companies use mold plates.
- Internal Candida is yeast that can overgrow in the colon. Test for internal Candida.

Dr. Feldman spoke about different allergy tests. Here is what we learned:
- The AICAT test is expensive and only goes so far.
- The cytotoxic test for food allergies is less than desirable. It doesn't do enough.
- The prick/scratch test is better than others, but still does not do enough.
- The intradermal/provocation is a beneficial food allergy test.
- Electro Acupuncture tests meridians.
- Homeopathy uses a system of dilutions with a mother

        tincture of the allergen, to combine solution in a vile. It is for immune system and allergy function.

- A good way to reveal food allergies is to eat no wheat or other possible allergen for six to 10 days. After six to ten days eat the food again in small amount and see how you feel. If you get unpleasant effects, you have an allergy.
- If you have a low allergy or sensitivity to a food, you can have a four-day rotation with that food and eat it only in small amounts.

Many experts were brought into this group to help with our self-healing goals. I would make it a point to see each expert who came in to lecture as soon as possible.

Luanne Pennesi, RN, MS, is a great person to work with in Gary Null's network. She'll call you out on your self-defeating bullshit in a hot minute, then guide you in a way only she can toward self-empowerment. She is a genius in what she does, and another person I hold in high esteem as a mentor.

Dr. Howard Robins is a world leader in a therapy called Intravenous Ozone Therapy (IOT). Disease cannot live in a high alkaline and/or oxygen environment. Ozone is a gas created by adding one extra nitrogen molecule to oxygen. This gas is non-toxic and acts as a pathogen scavenger in the body. It removes heavy metals, bacteria, viruses, and all impurities from the body. You must take probiotics with this treatment to replenish the good bacteria it may have killed. Because I had trouble walking, I was a perfect candidate for Dr. Howard Robins' study for IOT. There is a lot of literature on this topic that you can read for yourself. I can tell you that it made a tremendous difference in how I felt.

Another expert I met through the group is energy healer and acupuncturist, Bobby Aduna. He knows how to help you stop feeling emotions that are counterproductive to healing. Emotions that are out of balance can be just as debilitating as toxic pathogens, since the body responds to feelings by releasing chemicals. Negative body chemicals are disease processes in motion. It's really very simple: The more content you are, the greater potential you have to be truly healthy.

Donna Briggs specializes in colon hydrotherapy. She taught me the importance of a clean colon. I had no clue that most of us are walking around with at least three days' worth of crap in us. How can you detox if toxins cannot leave your body in an efficient way? Helping your intestines to work better will make your body detoxify faster. This is a no-brainer. She stressed the importance of chewing food properly and sitting down to eat in a relaxed manner.

I made several trips to Donna's office in New York City, which were really no big deal. She had me rest on my side, then gently inserted a tube in my rectum to receive the waste. Gentle massage and acupuncture accompanied the procedure for greater comfort. There was no bad smell because she keeps everything isolated. And she's so professional, the awkwardness really dissipates quickly. Our culture is way too skittish about bodily functions. It's time to get over it—our health depends on it.

I went to a holistic dentist whom shall remain nameless to remove my mercury fillings. To find an accredited dentist in your area visit the website www.IAOMT.org

Finally, there was hypnotherapist Dr. Michael Elner. He taught me that we can easily change the feeling we have toward something by changing our point of view or perspective. This can be particularly powerful for someone experiencing illness, loss, relationship trouble, or a career change. How we look at a situation changes that situation entirely.

In addition to the handouts my group was given, I took a bunch of notes:

- Luanne suggested mixing powder supplements with organic coconut milk because it is truly delicious.
- You will score your changes over time. Best to start your protocol in sections, otherwise it can be harsh on your body.
- People with cerebral issues tend to have stuck energy, therefore you must exercise. Keep an exercise journal to record what you do and for how long. Try to include both resistance and aerobic training in your routine.
- Supplements – green chlorophyll. I was already on a supplement program, and was instructed to add this.
- Juice recipe: Clean all veggies with veggie wash and filtered water first. Juice celery, four cucumbers, four lemons, four apples, cabbage, fennel, and spike with green powder.
- Have green powder with juice or coconut water every day.
- Red chlorophyll/red powder repairs the cells.
- Take vitamin C all day long. It is an anti-oxidant that gets rid of free radical damage.
- Take quercetin with vitamin C. It is a bioflavonoid. It protects cells from damage.
- Take protein powder every day. Add the red powder to it.
- Take Age Buster. It protects the brain and body.
- The bulk of your diet should be plants, nuts, and seeds.
- Take a fiber powder that is friendly for bowel cleaning. Mix Celtic sea salt into it.
- Take concentrate berries. You can take them with protein powder.

Gary ended the session with a lesson on the Law of Compensation. The Law of Compensation means to exceed the energy of your problem with ample vitamins and nutrients. At any level that you have exposed your body to anything unhealthy, you must take double the vitamins and nutrients to counter balance. This is where healing begins.

It's an uphill battle. Our environment is already saturated with poisons, from toxins and unclean air to radiation. Add to that our own poor attitudes and insufficient stress management. Would you believe that simply changing your diet is enough to reverse any disease brought on by all that exposure? For it to work, you have to flood the body with all the necessary vitamins and nutrients to the point that your body has no choice but to respond with a positive outcome. This is what the law of compensation is all about.

Part Eight: NUTS AND BOLTS

The following are notes from my support group, as well as from various readings throughout my treatment.

I trust that you too will reap great benefits. Note that as I said before I cannot give dosages of any supplement. And there is also a disclaimer: All the information that was given is not in any way to be construed as a prescription to cure the condition, but as a suggested nutritional component. Any information you wish to employ should be at the discretion of an attending physician. A patient's diagnosis, treatment, and medications must be considered to determine whether any of the suggested vitamins, minerals, foods, or herbs would contradict existing care or progress.

Special considerations should be given to pregnant and nursing mothers. Secondly, the protocol must be implemented in gradual steps. Begin with low doses of one or two items of the protocol's suggested items, and gauge the patient's acceptance and tolerance. Once it is determined that the patient has adapted, the dosage should be increased gradually.

The following is a healthy versus non-healthy protocol that helped me recover from my MS symptoms while also becoming a better person. Reprinted with permission from Gary Null.

Conditioned/Robotic Habits vs. Reasonable/Authentic Behaviors
Dead, chemically processed diet foods
Meat
Dairy
Processed foods
Caffeine
Soda, sugar, candy, gum Microwave ovens
ovens and stove tops
Cell phones/cordless phones protection on phone Smoking
smoking, air purifiers Alcohol
Whole, live
Beans, nuts, seeds, soy
Rice milk, Earth Balance Fresh fruit, vegetables, grains
Water, green tea, herbal tea High fiber snacks, dates
Toaster Wave shield

Non- Finding joy,

managing stress
Recreational drugs
Silver fillings, root canals biocompatible fillings
Not exercising
Living in stress:
detached involvement Personalizing worry
Fears
focused
Reacting with anger, defensiveness with positive action
Righteousness
Tolerance/consideration Cynicism, sarcasm
the opinions of others Depression and pessimism optimism
Rushing around
delegation
Adapting to dysfunctional relationships dysfunctional people
Living with financial restraints
financial freedom
Victims of chronic illnesses
optimal health
Dependent on AMA and FDA systems integrative therapies
Just surviving or existing
passion and purpose
Entitlement mindset
Empowerment mindset
Detached from environmental responsibility helping
environment
Drug free White
Activity Practicing
Creating goals Staying
Responding
Respecting Hope and
Paced time management,
Letting go of
Creating Creators of
Use of Living with
Involved with
Hand-outs from the Gary Null Health Support

• • • • • • •

Gary Null Health Support Group Template

- Introduction/ Overview What Influences Health Stress
- The Formula
- Creating and Managing Change
- The Mind/Body Connection and Chinese Medicine Principles Mental/Emotional Health
- Conditioned vs. Robotic Behavior • Life Purpose
- Behavior Modification
- The Immutable Mental Laws
- Neuro-Linguistic Healing • Laughter, Humor, Fun
- Physiological Health
- Nutrition
- Juicing
- Making Healthy Shakes
- Supplementation
- Healthy Fats
- Exercise
- Detoxify the Liver
- Detoxify the Colon
- Vitamin C
- Holistic Dentistry
- Natural Skin Care
- Bio-Oxidative Therapy
- Chiropractic Adjustments
- Supercharging the Immune System
- Balancing Hormones
- Suggested Diagnostic Testing
- Environmental Health
- Uncluttering
- Organizing Your Life, Your Stuff, and Your Time
- Cleaning Your Environment
- Personal Hygiene
- Recycling, Managing Trash

- Best Places to Live in the Country
- The Three Levels of Love: Self Love, Interpersonal Love, Transpersonal Love
- The Role of Activism
- Energy Rebalancing
- Balancing Chakras
- Clearing Auras
- Karma, Clearing Entities
- Receiving Intentions of Others
- Cleaning Cellular Energy/Releasing Past Pain
- Grounding Energy and Practicing Consciousness with Daily
- Meditation
- Kinesiology
- Feng Shui
- Reiki, Polarity Work, Network Chiropractic, Rolfing, Alexander
- Technique
- Oriental bodywork: Acupuncture, Acupressure, Moxibustion, Amma Thorapy
- Fiscal Fitness

The Energetics of Imbalance
Peace of mind and bliss are often equated with one's spirit. In Chinese medicine, we must consider that often imbalance starts at the least dense energetic part of our being; or the spirit. When the spirit is broken from a life circumstance, it often creates a negative emotion that we are conditioned to suppress, sublimate or deny. If we do not process the emotion and learn the lesson, the imbalance travels to the most-dense energy; or the physical body. By understanding the role each energetic layer plays it is easier to gain insights into self-healing. We always look at original cause or the root of the imbalance to heal it.

Our Spirit
- Our sense of connectedness to all things, to who we are
- Our purpose on the planet and unique greatness

- A sense of infinite, unconditional love and kindness
- Personal integrity, character and ability to commit to a deep purpose
- Playfulness, spontaneity, and the ability to express who we are • Focus, personal discipline, self-control and consistency
- Ability to learn life lessons and accept new information in order to challenge/change beliefs and values
- Natural curiosity, sense of awe, appreciation and gratefulness for all we have
- Our natural radiance
- A passion to live life fully and well, leaving a legacy behind when we leave.

Positive emotions and life events validate our values and feed our spirits. Enjoy them. When the spirit is broken, we are called to address it when we experience negative emotions.

Negative Emotions
Anger, anxiety, guilt, worry, rage, frustration, fear, depression, grief, angst, jealousy, apathy
Health promoting response

- Negative emotions need to be processed to repair the broken spirit; i.e., let them serve to motivate to make a necessary change to return to peace of mind or invoke your inborn "warrior" energy, which is designed to stand up for universal justice. Once this is done, allow yourself to let the negative emotion go and keep the life lesson/revelation.
- There is no stress in life. There is good information and the rest is live entertainment while you experience an adventure or life circumstances. The dramas we create around life events and the power we give others over our psyche is what makes us react to not being in control, asserting our learned dysfunctional behaviors. The key is to learn the skill of "detached involvement." Be involved in the event without tethering your identity to it.

- Bring with you your new lesson and wisdom; leaving the experience and negative emotions behind you where they belong.

Health Destroying
- We lose our personal identity when we use tools we were conditioned to use to deal with negative emotions: denying them through overwork, holding on to clutter, or
- justifying them via intellectualizing; suppressing them through depression, "grin and bear it" effect, and/or martyrdom; sublimating them through food, drugs, alcohol, gossiping, complaining, smoking, taking medications, projecting our stuff on others (blame, destructive criticism, defensiveness, righteousness, being judgmental), codependent relationships, sports, television, computer games, shopping, pornography, gambling.

Consumerism in our society is built on sublimation of emotions vs. processing them

"When the abnormal becomes common, it is normal."

According to Gary Null, "Consensus implies validity or accepted truth; however, to become healthy you must go beyond what our society calls "truth." It is carefully created illusion to influence your perceptions of what you accept as "reality" ... or not. A "consensus" is an accepted truth, but it could be based on flawed information. Universal truth sustains itself. Illusion supports itself with dysfunctional energy and cannot endure in the long run.

Physical Symptoms

We often get this information when there is unresolved negative emotional energy, along with any combination of unhealthy lifestyle choices that challenge the body's innate ability to function on our behalf. Left unresolved, negative emotional energy goes to the physical plane, which eventually affects our ability to function, to get our undivided attention. Every cell responds to every emotion you carry, especially the immune system.

Lung/Sinus/Colon Problems: Grief issues with the impermanence of the universe or initiated change, letting go, shallow breathing.

Digestion/Muscle Problems: Over-analysis; intellectualization; over studying; anxiety; worry; needing to be right, the best, or perfect to have love, acceptance, and recognition.

Heart/Circulation/Stomach Problems: Anxiety, apathy over joy, "What's the use?" and/or "Why bother?" and pessimism.

Liver/Gall Bladder/Tendon/Eye Problems: Fears (especially fear of failure/rejection), indecision, phobias, holding back, and/or not wanting to be vulnerable.

Breast Problems: Issues about nurturing, being nurtured, and/or abandonment issues.

Pelvic Problems: Also issues of nurturance; more related to initiating or birthing new things/ideas.

Immune Problems: Usually issues of the liver and/or digestion.

A great reference for this is Louise Hay's 1988 book, *Heal Your Body,* or refer to any traditional Chinese medicine textbook.

Juicing for Detoxification: chlorophyll juices green vegetable juice

10 to 16 oz. each

Basic guideline: Start out with one juice per day for one month. Then increase by one juice per day each month until the sixth month, and then begin to subtract one juice per day per month.

You can increase the number of juices you take based on how you feel your body is handling them. Feel free to add spices and sweeteners for taste.

• Juice 2 oz. dark green and 2 oz. light green vegetables. Add 6 oz. fluid such as a milk substitute, cooled herb tea, diluted vitamin water, organic fruit juice or filtered water.
• One tablespoon of green chlorophyll powder, add 6 to 10 oz. fluid (as above).
Sample juicing schedule: To make it easy to have fresh green juices each day, try making about a gallon of juice each week from:
• 1 bunch organic celery
• 1 bunch organic parsley
• 4 organic cucumbers
• 4 organic lemons (or limes or a little of each)
• 4 organic apples
• optional: add cruciferous vegetables like cabbage, other dark green leafy vegetables (kale, chard, collards, mustard greens, arugula, spinach, bok choy), ginger, dill weed, fennel, scallions, onions, garlic, mint, cilantro and other natural spices/flavorings. Add carrots, tomatoes, or beets for sweetness, but limit the amount due to the high glycemic indexes if you have imbalances related to sugar consumption.
• Pour this into several pint- or quart-sized containers with lids, leaving enough room for added fluids and expansion once it is frozen. Add powdered vitamin C to preserve the freshness of the enzymes as well as any other suggested additives. Place green juice lemonades in the freezer.
• Before bedtime each night move one into the refrigerator where it will defrost overnight.
• The lemons and vitamin C powder will keep the enzymes fresh for 24 hours once defrosted.

• Next day, put it into a quart container. Add your green powders, aloe, and other powders and fluids such as water, juice, vitamin water, or milk substitutes. Shake and enjoy sipping a fresh green juice all day!

Sample guideline for shakes and juices
- Protein Shake: Every morning a good form of protein helps to stabilize your blood sugar. Use a blender.
- Protein Powder: One scoop of rice, soy, whey, egg white, hemp, or pea proteins
- Liquid Aloe Vera
- Berries: blueberry, cranberry, pomegranate, or black cherry concentrates
- Frozen or fresh strawberries, raspberries, blueberries, acai berry, or goji berry
- Optional to add: nuts, seeds, nut butter
- Dilute with six to eight oz. of milk substitute, organic juice, coconut water, or filtered water
- Red chlorophyll powder
- Vitamin C powder
- Digestive enzyme powder
- May be added to this green juice: bee propolis (powerful antibiotic), lecithin (source of phosphatidyl choline to support brain, nerves, muscles and controls cholesterol and triglyceride levels) L-glutamine (brain nutrient, energy source, healthy libido), essential fatty acids or oils: Udo's Choice, flax oil walnut/avocado/borage oils
- Green Juice Lemonade: Helps to detoxify, oxygenate and alkalize the body.

Every afternoon:
- Green Juice (see sample juice schedule)
- Green powders
- Liquid Aloe Vera
- Vitamin C powder
- Spirulina, chlorella
- Dilute with six to eight oz. filtered water, coconut

water, and/or organic fruit juice.
- Sweeten to taste with stevia, agave, or xylitol,
- Fiber Shake: A gentle cleanse for the entire digestive system while you sleep.

One to three hours before bedtime, use a blender.
- Comprehensive fiber product
- 1⁄4 tsp Celtic Sea salt (re-mineralizes the colon) • Red chlorophyll powder
- Liquid aloe vera
- Vitamin C powder
- Dilute with milk substitute

Nutrition General Guideline:
- No meat: Includes beef, poultry and shellfish. No swordfish, catfish, or shark.
- Non-farmed cooked (no sushi) cold water fish, three to four times a week (optional)
- Organic nuts, nut butters, seeds (have only fresh organic peanuts/pistachios due to molds)
- Organic, non-GMO labeled soy products (tofu, miso, tempeh)
- Quinoa (high protein grain)
- Mixed grains with beans (cook beans with seaweeds or lemon to prevent gas)
- Veggie burgers, soy chicken patties, sunshine burgers (made with sunflower seeds)
- Seaweeds are high in proteins and minerals, and low in calories. A few examples are wakame, arame, hijiki, dulse and kelp.
- Protein shakes
- No dairy: Includes milk, yogurt, cheese, butter, ice cream, and cream sauces. Nothing with "casein" in ingredients.
- Non-dairy milks
- No butter: use coconut oil, almond oil, Earth Balance spread, or Spectrum spread instead.
- No ice cream: use rice ice cream or soy ice cream

without added sugar. Add berries, cinnamon/nutmeg, coconut flakes, carob chips, or ground nuts.

- No cream: use soy or coconut cream
- No caffeine/no alcohol: Includes chocolate, black or oolong tea, coffee, wines, hard liquor, and colas. Replace with herbal teas, mu tea, twig tea, Japanese tea, grain beverages (Postum, Roma, Cafix), soy coffee, Teeccino, green tea, white tea, rooibos tea
- No sugar/artificial sweeteners, including maple syrup. Replace with stevia powder (alkalizes the body, doesn't raise blood sugar), agave nectar (from cactus plant), xylitol, organic kiwi sugar, organic raw honey, organic molasses, organic barley malt, organic brown rice syrup
- No carbonated drinks (sodas and seltzer): Replace with spring, distilled or filtered water, lemon water (mix organic lemon juice, stevia, and ice for a delicious lemonade!), fresh organic juice, iced herbal tea, Teeccino, or soy coffee, coconut juice or coconut water
- No whole wheat or white flour (because of gluten): Replace with breads, cupcakes, cakes and pastas bade from spelt, sprouted whole grains (amaranth, quinoa, wild rice), rice bread, manna, millet• potatoes
- Nightshades can induce joint stiffness if you have arthritis. Avoid white potatoes, eggplant, peppers, raw tomatoes, and tobacco if you do.
- No fried/processed foods: replace with steamed, sautéed, stir- fried, broiled, or baked vegetables and whole grains
- Oils for cooking: coconut, macadamia (best for baking), seed (mustard, grape, sesame, sunflower), nut (almond, walnut, hazelnut, peanut for low heat sauté)
- Oils for salads and to add to cooked foods (avoid cooking at high temperatures): • flax seed or ground flax seeds, extra virgin olive cold pressed, safflower, avocado
- Spices/flavorings: Herbamare is a good vegetable

salt; Trocomare is a spicy salt; Celtic sea salt; granulated dulse and other sea vegetables, like kelp, sesame seeds, organic wheat-free soy sauce, there is also coconut soy sauce alternative

- Make salad dressings yourself from olive oil, lemons and spices
- Healthy snacks: Beware of glycemic indexes if you are diabetic or hypoglycemic! Try baked soy chips, unsulfured dry fruits, dates rolled in oat flour, non-dairy ice cream, organic popcorn, air popped or in a nut oil, plain unsweetened granola, watermelon, healthy snack bars, various organic nuts/seeds with carob chips and/or coconut flakes, organic raisins, and natural chewing gum, like Peelu or Spry brands.

Some important considerations about eating:
1. Eat primarily during the day; have your large meal "ideally" between 1 to 3 p.m.; this is when the small intestine "chi" or energy is most efficient.
2. Have a light breakfast (tea/toast, unsweetened granola with warm rice milk, oatmeal, protein shake) and a light dinner (grains with a dressing).
3. Have easily digested foods in the evening if you are hungry (non- dairy ice cream, green juices, soups) and don't eat at least two to three hours before sleep.
4. Eat in silence and/or while relaxing. Meals don't digest well when you are emotionally charged, stressed, or rushed.

Spice up Your Life – What you use to season your food could help you live a longer, healthier life.

Certain spices are rich in phytochemicals; colorful compounds believed to protect the body's cells and decrease inflammation. Adding these spices to flavor your food protects your health and allows you to use less salt when seasoning—an added benefit for those who are watching their sodium intake, according to the American Institute for Cancer Research. The protection provided by each spice is different, so try to incorporate a variety in your diet. Here's a guide to some helpful spices that can add a nutrient kick to your diet.

Cardamom
What it is: Aromatic pods with a warm, spicy sweet flavor.
Why it's good: Contains limonene, an antioxidant that's believed to slow tumor progression and detoxify cancer-promoting agents.
How to use it: Since it's a member of the ginger family, it's great in desserts, baked goods and gingerbread, but also curries and pickled food. It's readily available in ground powder. Fresh ground pods have more benefit.

Cayenne pepper
What it is: A hot, pungent powder made from dried cayenne chilies.
Why it's good: Contains high levels of capsaicin, which is used in medical ointments for pain relief, also works as a digestive aid and may have anti-cancer properties, according to some studies.
How to use it: Make anything from gumbo to chocolate dishes hotter and more delicious with just a pinch -- a little goes a long way.

Ginger
What it is: A plant from tropical regions grown for its gnarled and bumpy root, which is used in freshly grated and dried powdered form for its peppery, pungent, slightly sweet flavor.
Why it's good: Rich in antioxidants and often used as a digestive aid; it also contains the antioxidants gingerol and zingerone.

How to use it: An essential ingredient in many world cuisines, use fresh ginger in stir fries, sauces and salad dressings. Dried is great for ginger bread and cookies.

Turmeric
What it is: The dried ground root of a tropical plant related to ginger with a pungent, slightly bitter flavor and intense yellow orange color that gives curry powders and mustards their deep yellow hue.
Why it's good: That intense yellow hue also happens to be a sign of its rich antioxidants properties. Contains inflammation fighting compounds called curcuminoids or curcumin, and studies show it may help prevent cancer.
How to use it: Rice dishes, egg or potato salads.

Cumin
What it is: Cumin is the dried fruit of a plant in the parsley family. It's aromatic, nutty-flavored seeds and ground powder form adds smoky character to foods without a lot of heat.
Why it's good: A good source of essential nutrients such as iron and manganese, cumin also contains cuminaldehyde.
How to use it: Fajitas and tacos, veggies, sauces, spice rubs, and marinades.

Garlic
What it is: A member of the lily family with a uniquely hot, pungent flavor and subtle hints of sweetness.
Why it's good: Affectionately called "the stinking rose" in light of its numerous health benefits, it's rich in manganese, vitamin B6, vitamin C and selenium.
How to use it: Sauces, salad dressings, salsas, and marinades.

Cinnamon:
What it is: Dried bark of a tropical tree sold as aromatic sticks or ground into powder with a mildly spicy, bittersweet flavor.
Why it's good: It has the health boosting antioxidant eugenol, which works as an anti-inflammatory agent, and contains limonene.
How to use it: Desserts, beverages, breads, savory dishes.

Cloves

What it is: The unopened flower buds of the evergreen clove tree picked when they are pink and dried until they turn brown in color, with a distinctive warm-sweet flavor and aroma.

Why it's good: A powerhouse spice that contains several phytochemicals, including eugenol, and important flavonoids that also reduce inflammation and decrease clot formation.

How to use it: Cakes, pastries, sauces, marinades, mulled wine, and spiced cider.

Fats in the Diet
- Why eat fat? 15 to 20 percent of diet
- Insulates the body and internal organs
- Necessary for the production of hormones that regulate the body's thousands of functions, including the brain chemicals the help our memory, cognition and concentration
- Protects the cell's membranes
- Keeps inflammation in check by regulating prostaglandin production
- Lubricates the joints and muscles
- Needed for the synthesis of our immune complexes • absorption of fat soluble vitamins A,D,E, and K
- Energy

Types of fats:
- Saturated fats: found in meats, lard, butter, palm oil, and
- coconut oil. Saturated fats turn solid at room temperature. The liver needs these to produce cholesterol; however, most of these are also the culprits that clog the arteries and lead to degenerative diseases.
- Unsaturated fats (mono or polyunsaturated): found in vegetables, grains, and nuts are liquid at room temperature and are vital for the above listed body functions. Get cold-pressed oils.
- Polyunsaturated vegetable and fish oils are the chief

source of essential fatty acids that which help the body by controlling high BP, the formation of prostaglandins, and monitoring what substances are allowed in and out of your cells. Examples are safflower oil, sunflower oil, sesame oil, walnut oil, flax seed oils, and fish oils, such as cod liver oil.

- Linoleic acids (alpha and gamma)
- Linolenic acid
- Arachidonic acid
- Monounsaturated oils reduce the bad cholesterol in the blood (LDLs). Examples of mono-unsaturated oils are cold pressed olive oil, peanut oil, fish, and avocados. They normalize the bad prostaglandin levels.
- Hydrogenated fats: this means that polyunsaturated fats are injected with hydrogen bubbles to give a product the look of more "bulk" and the illusion of an easier consistency. It makes unsaturated healthy fats into saturated fats, such as peanut butter, margarine, and many of our chips. Responsible for "trans fatty acid" build up which increases "bad" (LDL) cholesterol levels, they increase cancer risk and cause premature skin aging.

The emotionalizing of foods in our diet

In most cultures, food is equated with love and nurturance. So, when we have a life event such as a marriage, death, birth, religious passages, birthdays, or anniversaries, we equate more foods with more love. So, when we feel anything but love, we tend to reach for a food source we were conditioned to equate with love, acceptance, and recognition. This includes feelings of loneliness, anxiety, sadness, or extreme joy. We "reward" ourselves for a job well done with "love" food. This is how we came to rely on unhealthy foods to meet our un-met emotional needs. This is a thought pattern that needs to be reconditioned if we want to be healthier, happier, and live more productive lives. There is also a guilt cycle that kicks in when we get unhealthy from our emotional comfort foods, so we feel bad and unloved, therefore we turn to food, and the cycle continues. Learning to integrate more reason into our choices instead of reacting to or coping with an emotion with food is a valuable skill that can be life saving.

"As the common diet moves further from the soil, so too society becomes more dislocated and diffused" – Socrates, 470 to 399 B.C.

Three substances from our diet that create inflammation:

1. Acrylamides. Acrylamide levels appear to rise as food is heated for longer periods of time. Though researchers are still unsure of the precise mechanisms by which acrylamide forms in foods, many believe it is a by-product of the Maillard reaction. Acrylamide may be produced by the reaction between asparagine and reducing sugars (fructose, glucose) or reactive carbon at temperatures above 120 °C (248 ^p).^^

A study by the USPDA proposed a mechanism that involves asparagine. Which, when heated in the presence of glucose, forms acrylamide. Based on current stage of knowledge, acrylamide is a natural by- product that forms when certain carbohydrate-rich foods are fried, baked, or roasted at high temperatures above 120C. Acrylamide causes cancer in rats when administered orally in high dose experiments, increasing tumors in the nervous system, oral cavity peritoneum, thyroid gland, mammary gland, uterus, and clitoris. There is a margin of 900-fold between human exposure to acrylamide in the diet and the dose that gave cancer to 10 percent of rats.

Raw, dried, and pickled foods
Acrylamide in olives, prunes, and dried pears develops through another process. Genetics professor Joe Cummins suggests a link between acrylamide and herbicides such as glyphosate, citing studies which show that heat and light can decompose polyacrylamide, the thickening agent used in commercial herbicides, into acrylamide.

Tobacco
Cigarette smoking is also a major acrylamide source.

Beverages
Estimates for the proportion of acrylamide in adults' diets, coming from the consumption of coffee, range from 20 to 40 percent. Prune juice has a high concentration of acrylamide, though adults consume it in far smaller quantities.

Cooking methods that affect acrylamide production
Acrylamide cannot be created by boiling and very few uncooked foods contain any detectable amounts. Browning during baking, frying, or deep-frying will produce acrylamide. Over-cooking foods may produce large amounts of acrylamide. Acrylamides can also be created during microwaving. The PDA has analyzed a variety of US food products for levels of acrylamide since 2002.

2. Arachidonic Acid (omega-6, pro-inflammatory fat).

There are two types of fats that fall into the category of "good" fats. These are the monounsaturated fats and the long chain omega-3 fats. You get monounsaturated fats from olive oil, selected nuts, and avocados. Long chain omega-3 fats come from fish and fish oils. These are exceptionally powerful allies in your quest for a longer and healthier life. However, there are some fats you want to restrict in your diet. These are saturated fats, trans fats, and arachidonic acid (AA). I consider these to be really "bad" fats. Arachidonic acids are found primarily in fatty red meats, egg yolks, and organ meats. This particular polyunsaturated fat may be the most dangerous fat known when consumed in excess and is known as an omega-6 fat. In fact, you can inject virtually every type of fat (even saturated fat and cholesterol) into rabbits and nothing happens. However, if you inject AA into the same rabbits, they are dead within three minutes. The human body needs some arachidonic acid, but too much can be toxic.

Ironically, the higher your insulin levels, the more your body is stimulated to make increased levels of AA. AA is a long-chain omega-6 fatty acid. Enhanced production of good eicosanoids requires the presence of EPA and DHA long chain omega-3 fats, found in ultra refined fish oil.

Remember, ions chain omega-6 fatty acids (found in high concentrations in vegetable oils) are the building blocks used to manufacture "bad" eicosanoids. The balance of good and bad eicosanoids will be the primary factor determining your physical and mental health.

Fish oils are rich in long chain omega 3 fats. Central to my wellness plan are EPA and DHA. DHA is the needed fat for the brain; whereas EPA is the key fat for your heart and overall health. Ultra Refined omega-3 is rich in both.

Arachidonic Acid, balance between omega-3 and omega-6

Arachidonic Acid (AA) is an unsaturated fatty acid that the body uses to synthesize regulatory molecules such as prostaglandins (hormone like chemical messenger) and thromboxanes (involved in platelet aggregation and blood clotting). Unlike the bad fats such as saturated fatty acids and cholesterol, AA is a form omega-6 fatty acid, which is a good fat. Omega-6 is one of the two types of fats that are essential to stay healthy. The other type of nutritious fat is the omega-3 fatty acids.

Arachidonic acid (AA), gamma linolenic acid (GLA1), and linolenic acid (LA) are three forms of omega-6 fatty acids. Linoleic acid is converted to gamma-linolenic acid in the body and then further broken down to AA. Omega-6 fatty acid in the form of AA can be found in egg yolks, meats (organs in particular), and other animal based food items. The other two forms, GLA and LA, can be found in evening primrose oil, black currant seed oil, borage oil, and fungal oils.

Essential fatty acid deficiencies can lead to reduced growth, inability to fight infections, and infertility. Omega 6 or AA deficiencies are not as common in the US. A typical American diet contains 11 to 30 times more omega-6 than omega-3 fatty acids. The general balance between omega-6 and omega-3 should be 1:1 or 4:1, according to University of Maryland Medicine. AA can be consumed directly from meat but in excess it can be unhealthy because it promotes inflammation and therefore leading to several of the diseases described above.

3. Glycation. Glycation and oxidative stress are central to the damage caused by diabetes. Unfortunately, neither of them figures into conventional treatment for diabetes, which is generally concerned only with blood sugar control.

Glycation occurs when glucose reacts with protein, resulting in sugar-damaged proteins called Advanced Glycation End Products (AGEs), (KohnRR et al 1984; Monnier VM et al 1984). One well-known AGE among diabetics is glycated hemoglobin (HbAlc). HbAlc is created when glucose molecules bind to hemoglobin in the blood. Measuring HbAlc in the blood can help determine the overall exposure of hemoglobin to glucose, which yields a picture of long-term blood glucose levels.

Glycated proteins cause damage to cells in numerous ways, including impairing cellular function, which induces the production of inflammatory cytokines (Vright, E. Jr., et al 2006) and free radicals (Forbes, J.M., et al 2003; Schmidt, A.M., et al 2000).

In animal studies, inhibiting glycation protects against damage to the kidney, nerves, and eyes (Forbes, J.M., et al 2003; Sakurai, S. et al 2003). In a large human trial, therapies that resulted in each one percent reduction in HbAlc correlated with a 21-percent reduction in risk for any complication of diabetes, a 21-percent reduction in deaths related to diabetes, a 14-percent reduction in heart attack, and a 37-percent reduction in micro vascular complications (Stratton, I.M., et al 2000). High levels of blood glucose and glycation also produce free radicals that further damage cellular proteins (Vincent, A.M., et al 2005) and reduce nitric oxide levels. Nitric oxide is a potent vasodilator that helps keep arteries relaxed and wide open. Oxidative stress in diabetes is also linked to endothelial dysfunction, the process that characterizes atherosclerotic heart disease. According to studies, diabetes encourages white blood cells to stick to the endothelium, or the thin layer of cells that line the inside of arteries. These white blood cells cause the local release of proinflammatory chemicals that damage the endothelium, accelerating atherosclerosis (Lum, H., et al 2001). Diabetes is closely associated with severe coronary heart disease and increased risk of heart attack.

The Value of Diet

Fats and Fiber

While fast foods can greatly increase your risk for diabetes, a recent study showed that a two percent increase in calories from trans-fatty acids raised the risk of diabetes in women by 39 percent; conversely, a five percent increase in calories from polyunsaturated (good) fats reduced the risk for diabetes by 37 percent.

If nothing else, simply replacing trans-fats in the diet with polyunsaturated fats will reduce the risk of diabetes dramatically. Dietary fats that are considered to be beneficial include extra virgin olive oil, fish oil, almond oil, almond butter, avocados, and nuts; and seed oils such as sesame, pumpkin, sunflower, and flax.

Eating a diet rich in soluble and insoluble fiber improves insulin sensitivity and reduces circulating insulin levels. Fiber impedes gastric emptying and the passage of food through the gut, slows the breakdown of high-glycemic starchy foods, and delays glucose uptake into the blood. In a recent study reported in the *New England Journal of Medicine*, researchers conclude that a high-fiber diet significantly improves glycemic control, decreases insulin levels, and lowers plasma lipid concentrations in as little as six weeks.

Sugar

• offers quick energy, but too much can throw off the balance of magnesium and zinc
• acidifies the body, making it more prone to inflammation and infection, depletes calcium, dissolves B vitamins, which accelerates conditions like arthritis, gout, nerve and digestive problems, and accelerates infectious processes of bacteria, viruses and candida (yeast)
• diminishes your immune response
• is often the culprit in heart disease, high cholesterol, and skin problems
• causes irritability, depression, absent-mindedness, loss of enthusiasm, emotional outbursts, anxiety, obesity, diabetes, hypoglycemia, tooth decay, and gum disease

Healthy Sweeteners

• Stevia: liquid or powder. Use small amounts or you will get a bitter aftertaste.
• Xylitol: liquid or powder
• Gymnemasylvestre: an herb that blocks the absorption of excess sugars; plus it curbs cravings.
• Agave: cactus nectar
• Barley malt (from the grain)
• Rice syrup
• Blackstrap molasses has B vitamins, iron, and calcium
• Beet sugar

Vitamin C
Vitamin C is anabolic. It cleanses, detoxifies and rebuilds the immune system. According to the Nutritional Science literature, its importance includes the following:
• Production and protection of connective tissue with the formation of collagen.
• It is an antioxidant, along with vitamin E, vitamin A, and selenium, to help protect cell membranes from free radicals.
• It protects cell membranes from viral invasion by stimulating T-cell activity.
• It helps regulate the amount of oxygen in cellular tissues.
• It helps in the absorption of iron.
• It decreases the need for insulin by strengthening the insulin producing cells of the pancreas.
• It helps in the manufacture of phenylalanine and tyrosine, which are important to our central nervous system.
• It helps in the transformation of the araurjo acid tryptophan into serotonin (neurotransmitter) for proper nerve impulse transmission.
• It helps calcium metabolism in teeth and bones.
• It produces thyroxin for the thyroid gland as well as adrenaline and noradrenaline for the adrenal glands, all of which are important for the management of stress.
• It helps with the common cold, diabetes, cataracts, gallstones, kidney stones, backache, stress, skin conditions, viral infections, drug addiction, alcoholism, cardiovascular disease, and cancer.
• It helps protect white blood cell walls from bacteria by activating interferon.

• It functions similar to antihistamines (breaks down histamine) and therefore alleviate allergy symptoms. It helps asthma by improving lung function.
• It prevents cataracts as well as helps to decrease intraocular pressure as seen in glaucoma.
• It helps to heal otitis and prevents gingivitis.
• It prevents and treats conjunctivitis, irititis, and uveitis. There is 25 percent more vitamin C in the aqueous humor of the eye than in the blood plasma.
• It strengthens spinal discs and decreases back pain.
• It helps in the healing of wounds, rashes, and burns by reducing pain, promoting connective tissue repair, promoting capillary budding, and reducing fluid buildup under the skin, and poisonous substances on top of the skin.
• It helps reduce the effects of herpes and shingles by helping to fight the virus.
• It helps in mental illness, addiction, and alcoholism by reducing the effects of stress these problems cause.
• It helps prevent cholesterol buildup with fatty acid plaques by converting them to bile-acids.
•It thins the blood like aspirin, and helps the blood flow less viscous, and is therefore likely to prevent heart attacks. It also inhibits the secretion of prostaglandins which contributes to the inflammatory process. It helps to destroy cancer cells by preventing them from manufacturing enzymes such as collagenase and hyaluronidase, which destroy normal cells. It helps the body produce antibodies, lymphocytes, and interferon; and stimulates phagocyte and neutrophil production.
•It helps in slowing down the aging process of cells by combating the peroxidation of lipids, which is directly linked to cell degeneration.
•It acts as a mild diuretic.
•It helps with the toleration of heat.
•It helps detoxify carbon monoxide, sulfur dioxide, arsenic, mercury, lead, and copper, by complexing with them and allowing the body to excrete them.
•It exchanges for toxins in the fat-cells that have been absorbed. •It helps to control difficulties associated with menstruation and ovulation.

•It prevents the production of nitrosamines, the cancer causing chemicals formed from the nitrates put in foods.

•It prevents plaque build-up by inhibiting the oxidative modification of LDLs (bad cholesterol). Also, once plaque insults the vessel walls, prostaglandin production is stimulated which causes platelet aggregation and clots.

•Vitamin C inhibits prostaglandin production. This then decreases this activity.

•It enhances an intracellular material called "ground substance" that holds tissues together. Cancer cells have a hard time infiltrating this substance.

•It inhibits the secretion of prostaglandins, which contribute to inflammation.

•It contributes to the biosynthesis of the amino acid L-carnitine and catecholamines (epinephrine, norepinephrine, dopamine)

Movement, Exercising, and Work-Outs

Why Exercise?

•It increases concentration of oxygen in the body and increases energy. Viruses, parasites, yeast, cancers and anaerobic bacteria cannot grow in a high oxygen environment.

•It increases your metabolism, endurance and strength.

•It moves toxins through the organs of detoxification (liver, lymphatics) and elimination (colon, lungs, skin, bladder).

•It increased endorphin levels and balances serotonin levels, which enhance the mood.

•In Chinese medicine the tone of the skeletal muscles is a reflection of the efficiency of digestion, so the more toned your muscles are, the more efficient the digestion is.

•It is a manifestation of focused attention and discipline, two of the hallmarks of functioning from the higher, actualized self. •You set out to look fabulous, which makes you feel better about yourself!

How to Exercise

Set aside 30 to 45 minutes for focused attention on your workout. Have clothes to work out in. Invest in workout shoes/sneakers and proper equipment.

•Keep variety and fun in your routines.

•For the first three to four months, do three days of aerobic workouts, 45 minutes; and three days of resistance workout, 30 minutes. Then go up to one hour of working out a day. Split between both aerobic and resistance workouts.
•Workouts can be found on various websites and TV programs, as well as video catalogs, journals, gyms, and walking/hiking tours, or adventure tours in your area.
•Stretching before and after a workout opens the muscle fibers, enhances circulation, works the breath, prevents injury, and warms up the body in general.
•Aerobic/cardiovascular workouts: Spin classes, biking, rollerblading, skating, dancing, swimming, and other activities designed to tone the cardiovascular system.
•Resistance workouts: Circuit training, free weights for upper body and lower body, calisthenics, and abdominal workouts.
•Eastern Movement workouts: Qi gong, kidney rub, yoga, and tai chi combine breath work/meditation with movement.
•Combination workouts: power walking, swimming, Pilates,dancing, skating, Nordic track, Tae Bo, rowing, and most team sports.
•Bouncing 20 minutes a day on a mini trampoline offers a comprehensive lymphatic detoxification.
•Other creative workouts: Alexander Technique, hand exercises, and specialty videos for those with chronic illnesses ("Sit and Be Fit" and "Chair Dancing" are examples).
"Those who think they do not have not time for bodily exercise will sooner or later have to find the time for illness." Edward Stanley. British Statesman, 1S26-1893 References: "The Complete Guide to Exercise Videos": I-SO 0-43 3-67 69 \v\ww.collagevideo.com Step Six of Gary Null's Seven Steps to Total Health."Exercising I: Exercising Helpful
Tips on Getting Started and Sticking with It"

Tips to Stay Focused
1. Make exercise an important part of your life. We know exercise is good for our health and well-being. Regular exercise should be a priority in all of our lives.

2. Set short- and long-term goals. Setting goals is a good motivational technique so you can maintain your focus. An example of a short-term goal may be to develop a good habit by working out regularly for two weeks straight. Another goal may be to lose a certain amount of weight or improve muscle tone and shape. Your long-term goals should center on using regular exercise as an important part of maintaining a healthy lifestyle.

3. Take measurements. Create your own before and after advertisement. Weigh yourself and take measurements of your neck, chest, waist, hips, and thighs at the start of your exercise program. Write down the measurements. After 60 days of regular exercise, take the same measurements and compare the results. This is an excellent way to chart your progress.

4. Choose an exercise program that's right for YOU. Start slow if you are beginning to exercise and choose a program that interests you. Consult a certified personal trainer for guidance.

5. Visualize success. Picture yourself finishing a workout and feeling good about it. Visualize achieving your goals by living a healthy lifestyle. If you believe it, you can achieve it.

6. Keep a journal. Write down your goals, personal experiences, workouts, and progress.

7. Use the buddy system. Studies have shown that people who make exercising a social activity stick with it longer. Encourage a spouse, friend, or co-worker to join you when you work out.

8. Vary your workouts. Use your imagination to keep your workouts interesting. Create a workout music soundtrack with your favorite songs. Change the environment from time to time. Exercise with different people. Take a fitness class. Play a sport that is new to you.

9. Challenge yourself. After you exercise, tell yourself you are good today. Challenge yourself to be even better tomorrow. The challenge will keep you focused and help you reach your goals.

10. Reward yourself. Take credit for the good things that you have accomplished. After reaching a goal, treat yourself by purchasing a new outfit or going for a massage at the spa.
Complete Health Network, Inc. Copyright © 2002

Supplements
Please note, you are encouraged to work with a licensed nutritionist in order to customize your supplement protocol. What follows is information drawn from the current Nutritional Science literature and is meant to be used for informational purposes only.

* Grape seed extract. Flavanoid with supreme anti-oxidant activity. Also recycles vitamin C in the body and protects brain and liver, and repairs connective tissue. Exceptional anti- inflammatory and anti-aging supplement.

* NAC (N-Acetyl Cysteine). An amino acid needed to produce glutathione, potent detoxifier of alcohol, tobacco smoke, and environmental pollutants, all of which suppress the immune system. It boosts protective enzymes that protect the body from aging.

* Alpha Lipoic Acid. Also a recycler of vitamin C in the body and a potent anti-oxidant. It deactivates free radicals and works well with Coenzyme Q10 (CoQ10). It also is part of glutathione production. It controls blood sugar and helps with nerve regeneration and reduces cholesterol levels. Found in spinach and broccoli.

* L-Carnitine. Provides cellular energy for the muscles and protects the heart. Enhances the effectiveness of vitamin C and vitamin E and is excellent to aid in weight loss with regular exercise.

* Coenzyme Q10. Extremely important for the creation of cellular energy, it is a significant immune system booster and increases circulation. A potent antioxidant that helps to maintain flexibility of cellular membranes.

* High potency multi-vitamin. Follow directions on bottle.

* Quercetin. A potent bioflavonoid, it is an anti-oxidant, anti-inflammatory, and anti-allergy supplement. It stops cancer cell production and tumor formation, inhibits free radical damage and prevents blood clots. It is found in garlic, chlorella, and dark berries.

* Sea Veggie Salad Capsules. Loaded with minerals and a great source of protein for the body without a lot of calories, they promote an alkaline environment in the body and are high in carotenes (vitamin A) and a good source of iodine.

* Carnosine. A superior brain cell protector that rejuvenates cells and protects them from premature aging; protects the chromosomes, and lowers cholesterol.

* Super antioxidant formula (or any high potency anti-oxidant complex). Overall prevention of disease and aging. Includes many of these: alpha lipoic acid, CoQ10, gingko, selenium, bilberry, cucurmin (turmeric), grape seed extract, zinc, burdock, bioflavonoids, green tea, vitamin E, vitamin C vitamin A, garlic, and proanthocyanidins.

* Cayenne tablets (follow directions on bottle). Dilates blood vessels, prevents blood clots, lowers cholesterol, immune stimulant, anti-cancer, antibiotic, and anti-viral. Cayenne enhances circulation and is a catalyst for garlic.

* Calcium Magnesium. Protects bone and teeth, helps with healthy blood clotting, nerve conduction, muscle contraction, lowers cholesterol, essential for bone growth, provides energy, and prevents muscle weakness.

Environmental Health/Environmental Hygiene

• Air filter; mini ozonators/ionizers, and/or automobile air purifiers.
• Water filtration, shower filter: under or above sink filters or at water main.
• Household cleansers: Use natural/organic products that are planet friendly (example: Citrasolve, Simple Green)
• Use peroxide for fixtures, tiles, and shower curtains. Use Murphy's Oil soap for wood floors.
•Use rubbing alcohol for floors and surfaces. To keep them disinfected use vinegar for mirrors and glass. Use baking soda or Bon Ami for scouring/scrubbing.
• Use laundry "magnets" and papaya bleach in laundry or planet-friendly detergents
• Use diluted bleach solution (1:10) to clean floors and surfaces. Remove wall-to-wall carpets which may have houses mites, their droppings, and microbes). Use a vacuum cleaner with HEPA filters.
• Natural linens and clothing vs. synthetics. Don't keep old pillows unless they are cleaned and disinfected regularly due to the collection of dust mites and their droppings, which build up over the years, especially in down products.
• Hardwood products vs. pressed wood and synthetics.
• Full-spectrum lighting.
• Duct cleaning if there is forced hot air heat in the home.
• Minimize electromagnetic fields in the home.
• No microwaves.
• Don't keep electric clocks or stereos next to the bed. Unplug appliances when they are not in use.
• Have everyone remove their shoes before entering your home to minimize the spread of microbes. Use shoe covers or have bleached flip-flop sandals available if people do not want to walk around barefoot.
• Have a cell phone shield for hand-held cell phones or cordless phones to prevent brain tumors.
• Pots and pans: glass/Pyrex, stainless steel, porcelain or cast iron.
• Remind everyone to keep the toilet seat down to prevent the spread of microbes.
• Be careful using synthetic candles. Burn only natural beeswax, soy, or coconut-based candles.

• Avoid irradiated foods and spices; and food colorings, additives and preservatives.
• Have your home checked for radon, lead, and asbestos.
• Use low-radiation computer screens.
• Avoid keeping a lot of glues and paint thinners in the house.
* Be alert to the microbes your pets bring into the house. Clean their paws when they come into the house from outside. Keep their coats clean. Find a holistic vet. Bathe your pets regularly. Use organic dry cleaners.
* Re-use bags when going to the grocery store or use cloth bags and insulated bags for your items. This will save natural resources, reduce toxicity of waste, and reduce costs for businesses and communities.

Natural pest control
• Sprinkle Borax around periphery of house to prevent ants.
• Plant peppermint around the house.
• Use technical boric acid for roaches and silverfish. Plant basil plants in and around the house to keep mosquitoes away.
• Cloves and orange peels repel flies.
• Clean all fruits and vegetables.
• Commercial liquid cleansers from the health food store. Clean and rinse one tsp. food grade peroxide to one gallon of filtered/spring/distilled water. Soak for five minutes and rinse with water.
•One cup of apple cider vinegar to one gallon of water (as above).
•One tsp. Clorox bleach to one gallon of water (as above).

Some ways to save our planet
•Always buy organic. You will be helping to eliminate harmful chemicals in the environment and you will be having nutrient-rich foods vs. those grown in depleted soil.
•Recycle and re-use whenever possible. Buy from thrift shops and secondhand stores.
• Eliminate unnecessary packing. Buy in bulk whenever possible. Use a water filter vs. plastic bottled water.

•Replace incandescent bulbs with CFLs and LEDs. Turn off lights and unplug electrical appliances when not in use. Consider solar powered attic fans, water heaters, and outdoor lights. Fix leaking faucets.
•Maintain your car. Rotate your tires often, get tune-ups, and drive slowly. Consider public transportation and/or walk whenever possible.
•Plant a garden or indoor herbs. Find sustainable land. Use organic/heirloom seeds and use mulch or grass clippings to reduce watering. Go back to push mowers vs. gas powered ones. Enjoy local bird sanctuaries and botanical gardens.
•Take action politically. Contact state, local, and national representatives, and urge them to promote cleaner air, water, cars, and tax incentives for alternative energy sources. Urge them not to sign any laws mandating vaccines.

Personal Hygiene
• Deodorants: baking soda, green clay powder, crystal sticks, and natural deodorants
• Cleansers: shampoos, cosmetics, bath and shower products. Natural face-washes and wash with filtered water.
• Avoid cake soaps as they harbor microbes in a soap dish. Use pump dispensers.
•Toothpaste (peroxide, baking soda, sea salt, or natural toothpastes without fluoride or saccharine). Mouthwashes (no alcohol or saccharine).
•Soak your toothbrush in peroxide three times per week to disinfect it. Store toothbrushes and cups inside the cabinet to prevent contamination from the spray of the toilet.
• Electric toothbrushes provide excellent cleansing without stripping gums. Soft brushes with a circular movement are effective as well.
• Use a tongue scraper every morning and after each meal.
• Natural medicine chest/first aid kit: contents are individual. There are homeopathic medications, Chinese herbs, herbal tinctures, natural antiseptics, topical preparations, and cotton bandages, for example.

• Cleanse the anus with soap and water or use baby wipes to cleanse the anus after a bowel movement. Always put toilet seat cover down before flushing toilet.
• Avoid chemical douches. Use green clay douches for cleansing.
• Avoid the use of chemical hair coloring. Look into natural dyes and tints.
• Do not use talcum powder.
• Use natural insect repellents on the skin.
• High doses of vitamin C will preclude you from needing suntan lotions. There are also natural watermelon-based sunless tanners.
• Skin Care: Use natural-based products that use alpha hydroxy acids and fruit extracts. Exfoliate regularly, moisturize daily, and use sunscreen.

Sourcebooks:
Cleaner. Clearer. Safer. Greener by Gary Null
The Nontoxic Home and Office by Deborah Lynn Dadd
Home Safe Home by Deborah Lynn Dadd
Uncluttering Your Home by Donna Smallin
Any books on Feng Shui
Dangers of Food Irradiation by Ted Nelson, QRA-certified nutritionist

We have long pointed out that you should never purchase nutritional products that have been delivered to you or to a health food store by any carrier other than UPS.

UPS is the only carrier that guarantees they will not irradiate their packages. Now comes more nutritional news about the use of irradiation and the fact that irradiation kills the nutrient content of living source foods and nutritional products. There's a new plot underway to sterilize your food and destroy the nutritional value of fresh produce. The latest push comes from USDA researchers who conducted a study to see which method more effectively killed bacteria on leafy green vegetables like spinach. To conduct the study, they bathed the spinach in a solution contaminated with bacteria. Then, they tried to remove the bacteria using three methods: washing, chemical spraying, and irradiation. Not surprisingly, only the irradiation killed nearly 100 percent of the bacterial colonies. That's because radiation sterilizes both the bacteria and the vegetable leaves, effectively killing the plant and destroying much of its nutritional value while it kills the bacteria.

The USDA claims this is a huge success. By using radiation on all fresh produce, they claim the number of foodborne illness outbreaks that happen each year could be substantially reduced.

It all makes sense until you realize that by destroying the nutritional value of all fresh produce sold in the United States an irradiation policy would greatly increase the number of people killed by infections and chronic diseases that are prevented by the natural nutrients found in fresh produce!

The USDA, you see, has zero recognition of the difference between living produce and dead produce. Just as many folks do not recognize the difference between living source nutritional products and dead synthetic "nutritional" products.

To uneducated government bureaucrats, pasteurized, or irradiated vegetable juice is identical to fresh, raw, living vegetable juice. They believe this because they've never been taught about the phytonutrients, digestive enzymes, and life force properties that are found in fresh foods, but that are destroyed through heat or irradiation.

Even a simple leaf of spinach contains hundreds of natural phytonutrients that help prevent cancer, eye diseases, nervous system disorders, heart disease and much more.

Every living vegetable is a powerhouse of disease-fighting medicine. But when you subject these fruits and vegetables to enough radiation to kill 99.9 percent of the pathogens that may be hitching a ride, you also destroy many of the phytonutrients responsible for these tremendous health benefits.

This means that while irradiating food may decrease outbreaks of foodborne illnesses, it will have the unintended consequence of increasing the number of people who get sick from other infections (and chronic diseases) due to the fact that their source of living source nutrients has been destroyed. For many Americans, you see, salad greens are their one remaining source for phytonutrients. Given their diets of processed foods, junk foods and cooked foods, there are very few opportunities for these consumers to get fresh, phytonutrient-rich foods into their diet. By destroying these thousands of healing phytonutrients, irradiation will leave many consumers defenseless against modern society's many health challenges.

We suggest you contact your U.S. representatives and senators to tell them you oppose the irradiation of produce that has been proposed by the USDA.

If you have nutritional questions, you can contact Ted on his personal phone line, (210) 326-2705. If you get voice-mail, leave a message, and Ted will return your call. This is a free service for all QN Labs Health Activists.

Quantum Nutrition Center, 123 Jackrabbit Run, Round Rock, TX 78664 USA

Uncluttering From the book *Uncluttering Your Home* by Donna Smallin, 1999.

I. Easy start
- Sort mail daily.
- Get rid of expired medications, vitamins.
- Get rid of expired coupons.
- Donate old clothes.
- Toss out old make-up and sunscreen.
- Throw out things that are broken.
- Throw out old socks.
- Remove grocery bags.
- Toss out old calendars.
- Remove spoiled food.
- Throw out rusted tools.

II. How to get it going and keep it going
- Organize your car: trunk, glove compartment, vacuum.
- Find receptacles for stuff you can't get to and label it carefully.
- Create a yard sale box.
- Do things on garbage day or the night before.
- Do it when you're angry. This helps you make fast decisions.
- Don't part with stuff you love
- Have friends help.
- Work to great music; lighten up. Do it aerobically.
- Move.
- Have a cleaning/painting party.
- Give thanks for your abundance.

III. Places to donate your things
- Homeless people
- Salvation army
- Church rummage sales
- Hospitals, children's homes
- Libraries
- Women's shelters
- Senior centers
- Local stage play places

IV. Where to sell your things
- e-bay and other online places

- Consignment shops
- Advertise in local newspapers
- Have a yard sale
- Pawn brokers

V. Storage tips
- Label everything.
- Keep household chemicals outside.
- Index storage.
- Get clear watertight bins.
- Use under bed storage.
- Use hat boxes.
- Check container stores like Hold Everything, Bed Bath and Beyond, and Rubbermaid.
- Put furniture in storage.
- Use bike racks.
- Organize gift-wrapping items.
- Organize holiday decorations.
- Egg cartons make good drawer organizers.
- Shoe boxes and film canisters also make good storage.
- Get film boxes and photo albums.
- Accordion files.
VI. Storage for kids
- Use pizza boxes for their artwork.
- Have storage for their games.

VII. The Areas
- Car: Keep a garbage bag in the car; and a notepad, an overnight bag, a cooler, a tool box, and a first aid kit in the trunk.
- Closets: Get rid of wire hangers.
- Bathroom: Medicine cabinet, under sink, shower caddies.
- Bedroom: Have a bag for items going to the cleaners
- Kitchen: Hang things, use baskets, use a lazy Susan, clean out the refrigerator, clean under sink area, clear off shelf spaces, go through pots and pans, and organize the junk drawer.
- Living room: Organize movies and music.
- Office: Organize books and drawers. Wrap up wires.

• Basement, attic, storage areas: Use shelving. Make space for trashcans and recycle bins. Use large plastic containers for potting soil and seeds.

VIII. Systems to Use
• Calendars
• "To-do" lists
• Pay bills, file receipts, and have a place for tax info.
• Put things away at once.
• Use a week as your unit of time to complete things.
• Group errands geographically.
• Have a place for stamps and greeting cards.
• Have a message center.
• Keep a magnetic list for food items you need on the refrigerator.
• Maintain your answering machine/fax machines.
• Keep alphabetical files.
• Have a fireproof box for most important papers.
• Keep records of: pay stubs, deposit slips, bank statements, cancelled checks, bills, insurance, receipts, legal documents, and investment records.

IX. Benefits of Getting Organized
• You'll have more time and more energy for living, loving, and peace. You'll be more satisfied with yourself.
• Clutter means anything you do not have use for or need.
• Stress levels increase with clutter.
• Clutter takes the joy out of living.
• Consider feng shui; the home is alive and full of energy.
• With clutter, we can't find things. That creates stress and chronic illness.
• Clutter keeps us from actualizing our higher selves.

X. Why We Don't Un-Clutter
• No time.
• Emotional attachment to our things.
• Procrastination.
• You think you'll need it someday.
• You believe you are disorganized.
• Guilt (you were brought up by packrats).

XI. Some Tips to Help Un-clutter
• Set realistic time frames.
• Imagine you had to evacuate in 20 minutes.
• Write five favorite activities and when you did them last.
• Remember, it takes 21 days to establish a new habit.
• Start immediately; do it flamboyantly, no exceptions.
• Do one thing at a time and do it with excellence.
• Visualize order.
• Journal your success.
• Don't give up.
• Look at how you are using your space.
• No wasting time.
• Inventory what you own; do you need it all?
• If all else fails, hire an organizer.

XII. Incentives
• Clear out files each January.
• Make a project list.
• Set time aside each week for un-cluttering.
• Have a yard sale.
• Have colorful file folders.
• Hire a housekeeper.
• Start and finish a drawer a day.
• Meditate daily.
• Remember, you control the clutter; it doesn't control you.
• Straighten 15 minutes before bedtime.
• Stop buying videotapes. Take them out from the library.
• Only shop when you need something.
• Tell people you're un-cluttering and ask for help.
• Avoid collecting brochures, pamphlets, fliers.
• File daily.
• Limit the number of subscriptions you have.

Part Nine: PRACTICAL ACTION

As you can see, this was a lot of information to take over the course of several months. In the end, I had only one goal in mind: to radically change my diet and beat this disease.

When I began removing any foods that could potentially cause inflammation to the central nervous system, I thought I might be able to find the specific root causation of my symptoms. No one knows the true cause of inflammation for MS; but by eliminating one potential cause at a time, we get to observe how our bodies respond. As Gary says time and again, "It's all about lifestyle modification and making appropriate choices."

In keeping with my attitude about positive changes toward a different result, I had to turn the lifestyle change into a game. I made my new diet something I could play around with and help me handle it without having a complete meltdown. Changes can be difficult. I needed to mentally prepare.

Before I could fully embrace the protocol, personally I wanted to say goodbye to my old diet with a bang. I went completely crazy with all my old indulgences for one more week. It wasn't easy at first to give up my gluttonous ways. Plenty of the foods that were bad for me were also the ones I most loved the taste of.

My favorite sandwich was a pork roll, sausage patty, egg, cheese, and deep-fried hash brown on toasted and buttered rye bread with pepper and ketchup. I'd eat two instead of one.

I maxed out on fast food sandwiches, pork rinds, and pretzel-covered hotdogs. Going healthy would certainly be a change. When that week was over, so were 80 percent of my bad eating habits. I say 80 percent because at that point there was still more to learn. My mental trick was to tell myself that I was eating from a new menu of life. It was time to try something new. This was an experiment of all experiments; one not for the faint of heart. Would this work?

The amount of healing we can experience is in direct proportion to our ability to change. I wanted to recover the best I could, for my own sake and the sake of my family. I figured if I followed through with the healthy living experiment and my symptoms still progressed, I could always resort to conventional medications.

Some people make changes one item or food group at a time. This approach is perfectly OK if you continue to progress. Me? I was impatient. I cleared out my refrigerator completely, giving some food away and throwing out the rest. After that, we went food shopping and made sure all the food in the house was protocol-approved. I carried a lot of food with me while I was out to lessen the chance of cheating away from home. When things got difficult and put me outside of my comfort zone, I asked myself: "Do I want to get well?" Answering "yes" each time made a tough choice less daunting. Once the choice for wellness is made, you simply do what you need to do.

I followed through with practical action. If a food didn't have a healing property, I stopped consuming it altogether. I took tons of vitamins and chlorophyll powders every day, meditated, and exercised. I did chelation, ozone therapy, Reiki, acupuncture, hydro-colonics, hypnotherapy, and vitamin drips. I stopped eating three hours before bed and de-cluttered my environment. I did these treatments as I learned about them in the group, one at a time, and kept going with each simultaneously, one building on top of another. There's a synergy that's created by doing this. All the therapies working in tandem improve the effects of the other. Again, I recognize not everyone can do everything all at once. Just do what you can. One at a time.

My body responded in a big way to all the changes—and fast.

At first, I did have a heavy junk food withdrawal. Not pleasant, to say the least. But I made the commitment in the beginning to do everything that was asked of me. I deliberately put my body through the shock. I wanted to feel the difference now, not later. I knew that if the protocol would work, the only way to find out was to do it all. Do you want to experience health slowly, at a moderate pace, or do you want it right now?

How many people change an unhealthy habit because it may cause major suffering later in life? Later in life is not now. No one feels the hurt now, so there is no incentive for most people to quit the behavior or bad habit. Even when we get old, *if* we get old, and the predictable symptoms manifest, many still don't bother to change. Why? Because by then we say, "Fuck it, I'm old and the damage is done, so why bother? We all die anyway."

Since when is this a positive approach? Living a long and healthy is not just a dream. You must choose to pursue it to live well. My advice is, once you choose health, do it in a way so you can push yourself without becoming anxious. If you feel yourself becoming anxious, pull back a little. This process may challenge you. Don't negate all the good you are doing with the diet with stress. The stress can cause inflammatory responses as well, so be mindful. Keep your life in balance as best you can.

Our bodies respond to the commands we give. When you believe "health," your chances are stronger to eventually achieve it.

Put yourself in alignment with what you want, because actions accumulate. If you've made the decision to get healthy, do what's in line with that. Eat right, exercise, and get enough sleep. Put what you want out to the universe and then let it come back to you. Have faith. Live in positive energy and action. Leverage your obstacles into advantages.

Part Ten: OBSTACLES

Lifestyle changes like this are a shock to physical systems. But these transitions also challenge and stretch your comfort zone on every level. The more fundamentalist you are toward anything, the harder time you'll have.

One of the biggest issues that people have with detoxing is how often they visit the bathroom. How else would you expect your body to respond? How often would you expect to defecate? I went to the bathroom so much I dropped 30 pounds in less than three months. Most people who eat unhealthy diets are not accustomed to defecating as often as they should. Most of us carry 10 extra pounds or three days' worth of fecal matter in our intestines. So, when a person who normally has a poor diet decides to eat healthy, what happens? They defecate like no other because they are finally giving their body the nutrition that allows it to detoxify. That's why hydro colonics are integral for their role in helping the body to eliminate toxins.

There are quite a few other obstacles along the path to good health. The first is food. Figuratively speaking, you've lived your whole life eating at the same restaurant, from the same menu. You've kept the same lifestyle. To do this protocol, you cannot eat at the same restaurants anymore. It's now time to eat from a different menu. But before you can change your diet, you must get your head right. You must prepare mentally. Thinking about your diet like it's a restaurant is one method that made my transition easier.

Making changes in your diet can also cause a lot of unintended drama from the people closest to you. This is because there is so much identity in food. You can lose friends and family members simply because meat is off the menu now. If you encounter obstacles with family and friends, which I certainly did, just remind yourself that another person's views on health and diet don't have anything to do with you. Just wish them well and do your best.

When it comes to family functions, don't get mad or upset when you're offered a hamburger at the next family barbecue. It would be in your best interest to adopt a "live and let live" mentality, even if it's not reciprocated. Focus on your health! Your family will eventually come around. No matter what challenges you face, get yourself a cheerleader—someone who believes in what you're doing—but most of all, believe in yourself. In some cases, you may have to walk away from your family for a time. Do it. It may sound selfish, but ultimately, you're doing this because you want to be around for the people you love.

It's a great idea to say a positive affirmation. For example, "my family is supporting me," even if they aren't, until they (hopefully) come around. Some relatives thought my wife and I believed we were better than other people because of the new diet. This was an unfair assumption to make; and when someone made us feel bad, our egos wanted to get defensive instead of simply explaining. A better approach would've been to ask the family members for their perspectives and have an open discourse.

Who gets healthy because they want others to feel bad about their own choices? No one. When a person is presented with an approach that creates harmony within the body, he or she may avoid the self-evaluating required. But it's impossible to grow when you are chained to former beliefs. Dealing with family might not be easy. The approach you take depends on the dynamic between you and your relatives. I know it can be difficult if you feel you're not being listened to or respected. Remember, you have the best intentions. They may too! It's not up to you what another person wants to put in their mouth. Respect others for their choices as you would like others to respect you. If a person is offended by how you eat, that is about how they feel. Not you.

Another option is to seek out places to go where you can find like-minded people for support. Even if you feel you're doing this all alone and the people around you reject these new ideas, remember we are never alone in this world. Sometimes it may be temporary and necessary to find solace in being alone physically. It's through spirituality that we learn we are all connected in ways we may not realize or readily see. As a dear friend once said to me, "None of us are truly isolated."

Another obstacle to getting healthy can be financial. Being able to afford holistic care may not be economically feasible. You may or may not need to go to extremes. Do as much as you can within your means, and always put it in your mind that you are getting what you need. Everyone can afford a positive attitude. Remember, what we feed our bodies is just as important as what we feed our minds. It doesn't cost any money to avoid junk food. And don't forget, exercise is also free—and vital.

Pay careful attention to your spirits and how you feel. Our physical, mental, and emotional systems are all intertwined. To turn over a new healthy leaf, we must cater to each and all systems for a holistic and integrated path to wellness. You may need some therapy like Reiki and/or hypnosis to help cope with the mental and emotional aspects of dietary changes. This is nothing to be ashamed of. Once again, pay attention to how you feel and don't be too proud to seek help if you need it.

We can be our own worst obstacle when we fall off track. It usually happens when we are feeling overwhelmed; opening a Pandora's box of negative emotions. If this happens, don't beat yourself up. Emotions need to be felt, recognized, embraced, and then finally let go of. Meditate, and use flower essences and essential oils to help handle emotions along the way.

Learn from each "negative" experience. Note that when I used the word "negative" I use quotations because if what you get out of the experience is the catalyst for your growth, then was the experience truly negative? The shock and change may hurt at first, but this is what happens when we shift our energies to better ourselves. Once we get past the shift, life goes on. Negativity is what we can sometimes feel when going through big life changes. What we are really experiencing is the destruction of what is old in order to embrace the new.

It takes tremendous courage to stand up and empower yourself with your own health journey. Many people are passive about their health at best, detrimental at worst. Once you decide to honor the temple of your body, make sure you don't neglect your mind and your heart in the process.

Part Eleven: LIFE FALLING APART INTO PLACE

Although writing about a relationship ending has nothing to do with reversing auto-immune disease, I found that telling this part of my story was important to include because the experience pushed and changed me in the most positive ways. Similar to leveraging a diagnosis to be a catalyst towards personal growth, so is any amount of adversity or life lesson. Life is taking us to class. Let's learn those lessons for the greatest of outcomes.

I was on my way to wellness physically but had done nothing to save my marriage.

Then my wife opened her first social media account. She was on her phone constantly. Curious, one day I looked through her phone and saw messages between her and a man I didn't know. My insides became Jell-O. My heart imploded. I confronted her, a bundled mess of anger, jealousy, disappointment and hurt.

I was determined to pay more attention to her, but it was the entirely wrong breed of mindfulness. She'd already switched off, and the more I pushed the more time she spent on social media. My jealousy festered and grew. There were countless fights. Before long I felt totally alienated and excluded as she increasingly sought solace from our marriage online.

Keeping my relationship together became about satisfying my own insecurity. Always questioning and wondering made me worse, which of course made her more distant. We were acting on our own hurt feelings and doing nothing to help each other, no matter how hard our egos convinced us we were trying.

One night an argument got so loud that I had to leave the house and go for a walk around the block. I was overwhelmed. My heart raced. It was as if I was being followed by a very large, dark energy. My brow sweated. I was overcome with panic and fear. I ran back home, terrified.

A few days later, we decided divorce would be the best thing for all involved.

Through all of this, I kept feeling like a train was about to hit my daughter. There she was standing on the tracks, unknowing, not hearing the whistling train behind her. I could see her there but felt helpless to save her. These images and thoughts ran through my head on a loop. My heart broke over and over. The most important person in the world to me was about to be ripped in two. This burned me like nothing else ever did—or has since.

The hardest nights for my daughter and I were our first nights away from home, away her mother. She just kept asking why we couldn't go back.

"It's not Mommy's turn to have you," I would answer, the guilt overwhelming as I watched my 7–year-old try to understand. Her crying on those first nights made me feel terrible. It took time to allow room for each of us to grieve: my wife, my daughter, and me. I had no choice but to live in the void. To allow energy to flow and heal, I allowed the pain to punch me in the gut and kick me in the face while I was down. I let the pain run its course.

Recovering from those emotions, learning to be a better man and father, and paying attention to all the physical ways to be well eventually all worked together.

And that's when the real healing began.

Part Twelve: MY RESULTS

My ultimate observation after all the reading, studying, research, and group work with Gary Null was that toxins in my diet along with toxic heavy metals were major factors in my inflammation and illness. You may find that your reasons for inflammation are different.

I eliminated all causes of inflammation, setting my body into healing mode instead of defense. And in fewer than three months, every last one of my symptoms disappeared.

It wasn't just my MS symptoms that disappeared, either. My acid reflux was also gone, along with several other minor physical ailments I'd previously suffered from and tried to ignore. My heavy metal levels went from being off the charts to below detectable. I understand not everyone can expect the same results. But my main takeaway is this: If you're going to heal yourself or at least make yourself as strong as it can be while fighting an illness, go all the way. Adopting an overall wellness regiment gave me instant results.

In case it may seem like one day I had MS and the next day I was cured, it didn't exactly happen that way. But it is undoubtedly surprising how quickly the body responds when we nurture it instead of neglecting it. It's the same concept as when you're used to eating healthy and then suddenly eat junk—you notice because your body will tell you. You won't feel good. The opposite is true when you don't eat well, and then start to eat healthy. Suddenly you feel better. Symptoms you've had (and some you only barely noticed until they went away), start to disappear. You just become better.

As far as I understand, the only difference between my symptoms and another person's is not where the symptoms are felt, but what part of the brain has been damaged. For the purpose of what I'm sharing, it would be self-defeating to say, "Well it worked for him, but it can't work for me because my symptoms are different." We never know why certain things work for some patients and not others. Every case is different. Each person's reason for inflammation may be different. However, there are core similarities for those facing similar symptoms to mine and the myelin surrounding the brain.

And no matter what condition you're in, getting healthy has never hurt a soul. However, you may need to do things slowly to give your body a chance to acclimate. Listening to your body here is crucial.

As I've said again and again, the primary cause for most diseases is inflammation. It is the cause for all autoimmune diseases, which are differentiated by where in the body the immune system is supposedly hyper activating. Whatever the disease, the premise is that the immune system is randomly attacking the body for no reason.

Inflammation is a localized physical condition in which part of the body becomes reddened, swollen, hot, and often painful; especially as a reaction to injury or infection. If autoimmune disease has caused an injury or infection, what is injuring or infecting it? When I stopped exposing myself what was causing my body to become inflamed in the first place, my symptoms stopped. It is that simple. Toxins were the cause, symptoms were the effect.

When the toxins are removed, the negative effects go away. One piece at a time with the protocol and you may find out your own inflammatory response. The protocol I used to reverse MS was the Gary Null protocol.

Most of us don't change unless we're faced with some sort of crisis. And even then, many of us resist anything different. My daughter was always my motivation. When she was born, I was nose-to-nose with her for a long time after she nursed. I feel tremendous love, and a responsibility to do right by her. She kept me going when she was just a baby. The same is true today. That young woman is my true north.

When you stop eating all the foods that cause inflammation, your body will no longer have a reason to respond to inflammation. When we don't treat ourselves well, our bodies respond with inflammation and illness. When we make healthy choices, we have more energy, less pain, we sleep better, and feel more at ease. In my case, we are talking about reversing a chronic illness—so even if my situation is not the norm, I am comfortable and confident advising you from my own experience and personal testimonial. We need to help our bodies do what they do best: protect us from harm, and heal us when harm comes from outside factors or our own poor choices.

When anyone is diagnosed with a chronic illness, it should not be the end of the journey but the beginning of a new one. To start on this new road, leave your baggage behind. The lighter your spirit and the better your choices, the greater your health will be.

This is your incentive.

When you do anything that is bad for you long enough, in some amount you can expect to manifest disease. This happens because the choices we make and the things we do accumulate over time. "Everything in moderation," they say.

When we expose ourselves to toxins over and over until disease occurs, can we say we've been in balance? Quality of life comes from where we prioritize. Actions and thoughts accumulate to produce either health or disease.

No one feels in balance during an illness. So how can we do anything that does not promote health and healing and still proclaim to be in balance? Even when we are not sick, we need healing. Even if you are on the perfect diet and have a perfect attitude, our environment is not always healthy. Personal habits either help or hinder us from healing, despite the elements we cannot control.

Our bodies can withstand significant damage before breaking. A diagnosis is an opportunity for us to stop and learn about ourselves. I suggest embracing a love of learning and curiosity when it comes to acting. It doesn't have to be laborious because it is all about what we bring to it. Be the candle in the dark room.

I believe that this protocol proves the way to heal the body is to flood it with everything good and exceed any level of disease. The fact that a person is ill may be due to negative actions that have accumulated. People have all sorts of reasons why not to do a complete and comprehensive protocol. You must choose. If you make excuses, you are not ready. Flirting with the idea with bits and pieces will not have the complete effect. Make love to the idea and do it with passion.

It may sound strange, but I'm glad that in the end I got the diagnosis. Living through this set the stage for me to become the man I am today: a devoted father, a diligent worker, a responsible businessman, and an attentive partner with a healthy, respected body.

My illness forced me to see the consequences of my actions and lifestyle.

Your body is your vehicle. And while most this book is geared toward physical healing, employing positive thoughts and loving yourself bring progress and the open flow of energy your body needs for healing.

My personal belief is that if your goal is to reverse disease, then keeping 100-percent to the protocol without cheating is essential. If you are otherwise healthy, the way that I choose to live is by employing the protocol nearly 100 percent of the time. If you do slip up and have something not on the protocol, don't beat yourself up about it. Just pick it back up and keep it moving. On occasion, I may eat or drink something not on the protocol for family events or holidays. These foods go right through me, then I'm back at it. If you're just starting, I don't recommend cheating at all for any reason. The idea is to cultivate the best possible routine in order to benefit your mind, soul, genes and cells.

It's been a decade since my diagnosis. Not a single symptom has returned.

SECTION TWO

Part One: GET OVER YOUR BULLSHIT

I spoke earlier about different obstacles we may come across that challenge our efforts in following through with a holistic protocol. I also talked about how stress can affect our well-being and cause our bodies to produce inflammatory chemicals. If Gary Null's protocol is about eliminating inflammation in the body, then it makes sense to take a hard look hard at what factors are stressing our bodies and minds—and to examine why.

There are good and bad types of stress. One releases damaging chemicals into the body, while the other produces "feel good" chemicals. A few examples of negative stress are feeling overwhelmed from too much multi-tasking, not meeting another person's expectations of us, not meeting a deadline for a job, and not having enough money to pay for basic necessities.

Positive stress is excitement. Extreme happiness, as awesome as it is, is also a strong type of stress. When we are excited, the brain produces happy chemicals like dopamine, oxytocin, serotonin, and endorphins—none of which cause inflammation.

Both types of stress are routed in extreme emotions. This isn't good, because it means we aren't grounded in our energy. Making decisions while not grounded rarely turns out well. The "feel good" chemicals produced in the brain are great to experience, I just don't recommend making any major decisions while under their influence.

So, what can we do about all this?

The opposite of stress is grounded contentment: happiness.

We conquer stress by creating happiness. And we do that by cultivating enough self-awareness to get out of our own way. Being centered and mindful of our own emotions will eliminate most of the daily roadblocks we run into. When you know yourself, you know your triggers. And that will teach you to stay away from unhealthy relationships, seek fulfilling work, and be your most loving self.

This is not dissimilar from the physical portion of Gary Nulls' protocol whereby we let go of what doesn't work in order to embrace something new that can.

Happiness is the goal, but happiness requires work. Every bit of effort we put toward ourselves and achieving even the smallest victories works like rolling the smallest of stones until it becomes an unbreakable boulder.

Part Two: SELF-AWARENESS

To reach self-awareness, you must first understand cause and effect. I first heard about this concept while studying Nichiren Daishonin Buddhism. To understand the effect of anything, we must first learn to recognize the cause. Are you living a life that is a mirror of another person's perspective? This person may be a parental figure, or any person who had a dramatic influence on you during your upbringing. Study the decisions you've made. Do you form choices from your higher, greater self? Is your voice your own? Why do so many people who are raised financially disadvantaged stay that way? There are beliefs unknown to the rest of us that subconsciously keep many from transcending to a higher life condition no matter how hard they try.

Conversely, why are there people who can manifest their dreams no matter where or how they were raised? A person's life condition is a space of energy. Gary would often state, two energies cannot share the same space. To make life changes, you must release the energy of what has been your existence. You must allow yourself to feel every emotion that comes with letting go of things. Prepare. Don't deny your emotions that come from growing. There may be some huge changes on the horizon. For each change you experience, give yourself time to mourn the departure of what you're letting go of. Feeling sad is normal. Fully embrace this emotion. Then, let it go. Make a ritual if you need to in the process. Then, let it go.

It is terribly difficult to let go of feelings, especially bad ones. But you cannot be healthy if you are not able to shift your energy in a positive direction. This is not to say we should be in any denial of a problem or challenge, but things can be easier to tackle with a positive outlook.

Life can be absurdly difficult and unfair. Even at its most trying, however, our only healthy option is to pick ourselves up and dust ourselves off. The help is there if we simply ask for it. Just keep picking yourself up, and eventually you'll get it. Trust that everything happens on its own time, every time. Keep working on your energy, and eventually you'll find that life becomes easier because you'll be able to listen to your intuition and do things based on intuition and not on ego. Listening to your intuition is like accessing the voice of the universe or your inner guide.

Trusting in this voice will always bear a positive result. Adversely, many people trade trust for a sense of control. But as anyone who's tried it knows: The more you try to control, the less control you have. Like the saying goes, man plans, and God laughs. Feelings of control come from one place: the ego, which is mostly wrong. The ego does have some positive functions. Control is not one of them.

Your intuition is never wrong. One way to get in touch with your intuition is through the practice of meditation.

Meditation is a practice of mental stillness achieved through outward awareness. It's not about quieting the mind. The mental stillness comes from the outward awareness brought on by being in the moment. When you can become proficient at being in the moment, the mind becomes still on its own. Simply put, it's just a shift in awareness. You're taking your attention away from your mind chatter and more towards your surroundings and happenings.

Meditation is a helpful exercise for working toward self-awareness and can help us be less reactive and chained to our emotions. You learn to let your thoughts come and pass through without attachment. Everything happens on its own time, every time, and so will your mental stillness. Achieving mental stillness is like turning down your inner volume knob. As things become quiet in your mind, your intuition becomes easier to hear and the less emotionally reactive you become. You're finally able to think clearly and respond to things from a place of love and stillness. Responding to things reactively takes us away from peace and, ultimately, happiness. Meditation is one tool in the toolbox.

I prefer to sit comfortably with my back straight when I meditate. I don't try to quiet my mind. I just become mindful of my surroundings. I allow my thoughts to pass through as I focus on my breath and relaxation. Over time, I begin to experience some disconnect between my mind and my body's vibrations, viewing myself in almost the third person. When this occurs, I no longer feel attached to my emotions. I can now be an observer from a detached, non-reactive perspective.

These days, I try to be the observer no matter where I am. If you meditate in this way, over time being the observer will come more easily and naturally. You may find that detachment from emotion helps maintain a state of calm.

To clarify: Detachment doesn't mean you suddenly become a zombie. Think of detachment more like emotional-self objectivity. It's a part of self-mastery whereby our emotions don't determine our actions. As a part of the human experience, there will always be emotions that can carry us away. It's what we do with those emotions. For now, we can simply refer to this way of being as detachment. Meditation provides a way to sustain happiness and peace in your life. Another way of looking at detachment is to say I own my emotions, but my emotions do not own me.

This detachment shouldn't be saved only for meditation! As it becomes easier to become centered in your practice (or through prayer, which is another form of meditation), you can bring this stillness out into your everyday life. Eventually that awareness can be with you in every moment.

Meditation can also be guided to focus on physical healing.

When you wake up each morning, stay in bed with your eyes closed and imagine yourself healed. Imagine your body completely well, healthy, and healed. Focus on this as you take a few deep breaths. Next, sit up and put your feet on the ground. Close your eyes and imagine roots growing 10 feet into the ground while a white light shines into the top of your head, through your spine, down through your legs, and down below your feet into the roots.

There are countless ways to use guided meditations like this for your physical benefit.

There are two primary culprits keeping us from mindfulness. One is conditioning through our upbringing. The other is emotional reactiveness. These two are good at playing off each other and sparking a reaction. That makes detachment even more important; and only achievable by staying present and objectively aware of your emotions.

Feelings originate in thought. Our mind is where everything starts and ends: the beginning, middle and end. What happens in our mind affects the chemical reactions occurring throughout our bodies. Emotions create the vibration sent from our soul to the universe, which in turn reflects into our reality. Certain chemical reactions can be damaging or healing, totally affecting our ability to be in the moment.

If you want a positive outcome in your life, then you must start with positive thoughts.

I don't imply that thinking a positive thought creates immediate change. It's a little more involved. The beginning of this comes from our relationship with ourselves. So, let's take a deeper look at that relationship. But what is the point of this exercise? Why bother working on yourself at all? The entire point is to take responsibility for your life and your pursuit of happiness. You can only manifest what you can cultivate within yourself. That's why it's good to work on the relationship you have with yourself.

All too often we look to for things and people outside ourselves to feel complete. But each of us is comprised of universal energy. You are already complete! Society trains us to forget that we have all the power we need within ourselves. We can remember. Understand that the emptier you feel, the easier it is for external powers to leverage your emotions against you for their own purposes. Emptiness creates a void that corporations look to take advantage of, and abusers prey on.

The relationship you have with yourself is just as important as your relationship with others. The integrated blend of your spiritual, physical, emotional and mental bodies determines your well-being. How you treat others reflects this. What we see in others is also a reflection. Every time we point the finger at someone, we have three fingers pointing right back at us. The antithesis to everything being wrong is a positive outlook. A positive life begins with a positive outlook, and our body systems follow the example we set with clear focus on a healthy routine.

A big part of this work involves tackling our own egos and self-esteem. Let's call this the "egoic mind." The egoic mind is a master liar. Capable of making everything all about us. Depending on the circumstance, this can be a helpful or very harmful thing.

But first, let's quickly consider the human condition in all this.

Our human condition is born in the primal/animal part of our brain. Ego is very much part of that, especially the negative ego mind and emotional reactiveness. This part of us generates automatic responses and opinions based solely on external conditions. It allows us to make snap decisions on what or who is safe for us or not. Only when we feel the connection to our higher selves can we tell the difference between spiritual intuition and primal/animal brain response. Both give us a sense of protection. Both can create emotion or caused by emotions. Detachment is one path. An example of how our primal instincts come into play are why we feel attraction towards people.

For many, this part of the brain is the driver behind the wheel in our lives. It allows for deception and manipulation. It allows for obsessive-compulsive behaviors. It allows for racism. The main concern is survival on the most selfish levels.

Words of the negative egoic mind might sound something like this:

I will put you down in such a way that it builds me up. You are less than I, and I am superior to you. The reality is that I feel like I am not enough, and therefore I put myself on a pedestal. I am drowning in insecurity. You don't know me. You don't know what I've been through. It's all about me. I feel empty and dissatisfied, so I need to manipulate you to validate myself, by making it your responsibility to make me feel special. I don't feel special myself; I need all your attention. As much as I require perfection and the world in my hand, I will do everything in my power to insure I don't get it. I can't get out of my own way. I am not worthy, but I love you. Please love me so I can take you for everything, because I am entitled. I own you. I do not believe or feel the abundance in the universe.

When you live in your brain, you live through the ego. And the primary goal of an ego is to protect from hurt—typically through reactionary behaviors of fear and self-righteousness. But avoiding feeling hurt avoids the lesson. Avoiding the lesson avoids growth. Avoiding growth avoids happiness.

This is all negative ego.

A huge problem with this thinking is that it becomes addictive and it is rarely conscious because the negative ego cannot see any big picture.

Words of the positive egoic mind may sound something like this:

I truly love and appreciate myself. I am not afraid to do what is in my highest good and without your approval. If you don't support me, I wish you the best. Seeing others excel lifts my spirit. Helping others be successful helps me become more successful, even indirectly. If I am not where or what I want to be, I can fake it until I make it. I see abundance within the universe. I visualize what I desire the most and do what is in line with that desire in a way that does not harm others. I can see the greater picture and do what is in harmony with the life I am working to manifest. I have faith in myself. I feel the power and value in what I'm blessed with to offer the world. I am filled with love and give love freely, without strings attached.

An applied use of this form of thinking is leveraging the "liar" part of the egoic mind. An example of this is when people say, "fake it 'til you make it." Let's suppose you're living a lifestyle that is not of your liking. A method regularly employed for improving ones' lifestyle is using the egoic mind's ability to lie to us about our reality in favor of a more attractive reality. This isn't a delusion of grandeur. This is a person mentally visualizing what they want out of life, and then putting out the feeling of having it with intention. This is a positive use of the egoic mind; one requiring knowledge of one's self-worth and a healthy self-esteem.

This is how I have awareness of the difference between the negative and positive egoic minds. I know what thoughts are worthwhile to entertain.

Self-love is vital to a healthy relationship with yourself. This includes making peace in your life a priority. It includes setting boundaries and defending them. It includes respecting yourself. Only you can set your own standards for what you allow in your life. Other people do not know how we expect to be treated. It's up to us to teach those who are in our lives what is acceptable. If a person isn't honoring our sense of harmony and peace, that is when you end the relationship. Learn to communicate effectively and directly.

Another part of self-respect is knowing when to say no.

Imagine you have a cup. We'll call it the Giving Cup. It's an excellent self-attribute to be altruistic. This is what the Giving Cup is for. It's one way we can bring abundance in our lives. The key, however, is to stop giving when your Giving Cup is empty. It doesn't mean you care less. It means you don't give what you don't have.

All these ideas can help with the relationship with yourself and keeping your life peaceful.

Now that we've explored the relationship, we have with ourselves and our egoic minds, let's dig a little deeper into the thoughts we entertain.

Self-affirmations are a great way to reverse negative thought patterns, which are the root of many diseases. Your thoughts steer your life.

Saying positive affirmations puts us in a place where lingering emotions can be released. To counter a negative thought, affirmations should be said three times. Follow this through by using what's called the Emotional Freedom Technique (EFT) to release the emotion associated with the thought. Fotini Pappassaves taught me this.

To perform this EFT, tap your fingers lightly on your eyebrow, call out what your emotion is, why you feel that way, and then speak out, "even though I feel_____ from or because _____ I still like myself, I love myself, and I adore myself." Next you say, while tapping, "I now release this feeling of _____ from _____, because I like myself, love myself, and adore myself." This kind of positive Mad Libs will release the negative emotion.

Continue to do this until you feel an energy shift. Let's fill in the blanks with an example. "Even though I'm feeling abandoned from someone close to me abruptly leaving my life, I still like myself, love myself, and adore myself." Continue to tap. "I now release this feeling of abandonment from someone close to me abruptly leaving my life, because I like myself, love myself, and adore myself."

Using flower essences and essential oils can help with this as well. You can purchase these at almost any health food store. Apply the essential oil to your wrist or steam them in a diffuser. You can also use flower essences by mixing them with water or dropping or spraying them in your mouth.

Do your best to avoid negative thoughts toward others or yourself because the energy you put out is the energy that will come back to you. Think of your thoughts as a boomerang. We all want positivity, and all it takes to get it is to share it. Any actions and thoughts you entertain have an accumulative effect. If you carry many positive thoughts and do things that are overwhelmingly positive, then you can expect a positive result. It is this concept that is the heart of it all.

When we indulge in negative thinking and behaviors, they manifest monstrously because of the bad energy we unconsciously allow into our space. The energy we entertain is the energy we invite. In simplest terms, what you give is what you get.

Trying to keep my attitude and emotions in check is a non-stop effort. You will never escape your ego or the little devil on your shoulder, filling you with doubts and what-ifs. The point is to act with what is positive. Just because you have an impulse to act inappropriately does not mean that you should.

We can change the feeling we have toward something by changing our point of view or perspective. This can be powerfully helpful to a person who would otherwise look at his or her illness—or anything wrong in life, for that matter—with a sense of doom and foreboding, like the world is going to end.

None of this is to suggest that you should ignore how you feel. To be released, feelings must first be allowed in. Allowing yourself to feel your emotions, no matter what you're reacting to, and acknowledging them is an excellent way to release them. Becoming mindful of your environment and thoughts is the first step in training yourself to be less emotionally reactive. It's not about controlling what you feel. That type of control happens over time with practice.

Do you lash out and become destructive? You need to ask yourself how you can leverage your negative emotions toward positive outcomes. Yes, you can punch a wall or make someone else feel bad. It may feel good, and yes, it is a form of release. The issue is that this form of release is egocentric and not of your highest good. If you continue to release your emotions in this way, you will never become happy.

You might say," I don't care about my next level!" But if that was true, you would not be reading this book.

Exercise. Dance. These actions help to release lingering emotions. Cry out loud—but never cry for too long, because crying has its own vibration that will mirror back to you and give you more reasons to cry. Instead, say positive affirmations to rewire your brain. Doing all of this ultimately helps you become a person who manifests positivity because it's part of your natural thought process.

Emotions create physical vibrations that send messages through our spiritual energies to the universe for what we want. Empathetic energy is why you can sometimes feel what someone else is feeling, but not think what they're thinking. The vibration is palpable. The universe feels it too. As your emotions reflect what you think, the universe returns what you are feeling. Everything is validated. This is where intuition is linked with emotions. It is only through detachment that we can separate our emotions from intuition because intuition is also a "feeling."

Emotions can be a valuable tool if we know how to use them. They can indicate if we are entertaining the wrong thoughts. They can tell us how or when we need to work on ourselves some more. They can be used to motivate us to change. Anger can be a great motivator when used constructively. But the way we carry anger and resentment toward people who have hurt us can also be detrimental to our health. If you feel hurt, let yourself experience the pain that comes with it. Cry it out, talk it out. Not all scenarios get closure. Therefore, it's important to focus and work on inner strength. To preserve ourselves, we are forced to honor ourselves by letting go. When you are ready, forgive the other person. Then go ahead and forgive yourself. Don't carry that weight too long.

Sadness is a part of growing when we let go of something we care about. Sadness, like anger, can take us away from the moment. Crying out loud can help release sadness. Negative emotions rarely take us anywhere good, unless we find a way to channel that energy for healing. But at first, it's OK to allow the emotion to run its course.

Fear may help us feel safe at times—but it also does the opposite. It is love that keeps you safe. Fear constricts, confines, isolates; it blocks the flow of energy and will never protect you. Have faith and not fear, for the love you hold for yourself and other people is what frees, opens, connects and protects you.

It's in your best interest to get into the habit of allowing yourself to experience emotions and then letting them go. As you practice, you'll get better at it. What better way to show your body how much you love it than by eliminating emotional toxins? Managing and repairing emotions is crucial. Continuing these practices creates a complete turn-around within you.

Because your body has the innate ability to heal, the best thing to do is to create circumstances that are conducive to that purpose. The hardest part is learning how to get out of our own way. Become self-aware enough to get out of your own way and nothing will be in your way towards achieving your greatest health.

Now let's explore the other part of this, which is our conditioning. Our conditioning comes from things that we've learned through authority figures in our lives and experiences. Our conditioning becomes reactions to things that are automatic. It's one way we are programmed. We've discussed how to release lingering negative emotions, but how do we release negative conditioning? A lot of us are angry at the people who guided us down the wrong paths that left us unhappy and unfulfilled. Forgiveness is the first step in releasing negative conditioning. We may need to forgive those who negatively influenced us. Many of us take issue with our parents and upbringing in one way or another. Sometimes our parents did the best job they could with the limited resources and skills they had.

For those who use their childhood family story to identify and maintain a victim point of view, consider this: There are plenty of people who are raised in worse conditions than you were, and they still become successful and happy. They pulled from those experiences and used them to grow strong. This is just like leveraging negative emotions toward a positive outcome.

Some people walk through life unaware of how circumstances shape their lives. These people ignore the essence of who they really are. Whether they know it or not, their lives unfold within a set of environmental circumstances.

Well, what if you were born under a different set of circumstances? Who would you be then? Would you be a different person today? Which part of what makes you who you are would be the same no matter what cards were dealt? What part of your personality is authentically you? Which part of your reasoning comes from your individual character essence versus what came from your upbringing? What part of you has nothing to do with your authentic self, and more to do with your environmental circumstances?

Negative conditioning is the baggage you carry around.

We did not come into this world holding bags filled with horror stories of how we perceived the environments in which we were raised. The baggage I'm referring to is the construct of our identity over time. To illustrate, imagine a baby sitting on a floor. In front of this baby is a butler's plate filled with ideas, fears, family, things to love, things to hate, and expectations. This baby is perfectly authentic as-is. The personality is already pre-programmed by its own unique energy. Ideas, things to like and dislike, and even talents and gifts are also pre-programmed. We are born with our personality and who we authentically are. The nature of who you are is already there.

This baby on the floor must consume the entire plate as it is fed to them. Some items are fed lovingly, and others not so much.

It takes a village of people to feed us the various things and pieces of life we absorb over time that contribute to our identity. A lot can come from parents, or lack thereof. Many of us blame what's wrong with us on what our parents did to us or didn't do for us. It all gets digested. Some things might be self-empowering, while others might be self-defeating. How can we tell the difference?

What is self-empowering will manifest itself in fulfillment and satisfaction of life. What's self-defeating can be a pattern that doesn't move you forward to something positive. The idea is to try to discern between your conditioned versus your authentic self. The bags you carry (holding all you've been fed) may leave you finding a sense of importance in being a victim and defended by the negative ego mind. Some use this to get attention from other people and gain a sense of validation.

There are no belief systems we are born with or attached to. Try to imagine having no belief system, and no preconceived notions or perceptions of life. Conceiving of this blank slate can be difficult when we are powerfully conditioned. Try it anyway. The point is to become open.

Now imagine being equally open to any possibility or opportunity in your life. This process will hopefully help you gain the strength to set your bags down, ego included. How light that must feel! How freeing, to not have any horror-filled bags to carry. Without heavy baggage, you can soar. It is easier to live with purpose, pursue noble intentions, and allow positivity to color and enhance your existence.

Imagine yourself in a place where you excel, instead of getting pulled down into a muck of negativity. Perhaps you've found a way to truly put your bags down. Not only have you put them on the floor and let go, but you are able to walk away and be free. You can feel light, unencumbered. You can walk with love for yourself because you've forgiven yourself for carrying those heavy bags. You can stand with your feet firmly grounded, or leap like you are about to hit the roof and soar into the sky. Never regret carrying those bags once you've put them down. Each bag represents a life lesson. Those lessons are important for us to understand. When we are unburdened and free, open to new ideas, operating on a clean slate, lessons can resonate and have a lasting, positive impact.

I say to you, drop those bags! Release whatever you've held on to for so long, and don't look back. There is no need to dwell. All that remains are more lessons to learn, allowing you to become a better person.

Letting go of conditioning on a conscience level is one thing. What about releasing subconscious conditioning you're not aware of? Think about the knee-jerk reactions you have to some things without thinking, and the emotions that come along with those reactions. Are there other bags you haven't put down yet?

One example is a simple misunderstanding. No matter what a person might say to you, you can respond two ways: appropriately, meaning your interpretation of what was said to you and the other person's intention fall in line, so your response is in context with the conversation; and inappropriately, meaning there is a difference between your perception of what was said to you and the actual message intended by the other person. The next thing that can happen is the person tries to explain themselves differently, but you don't care to listen because your feelings have been hurt, your ego damaged, and now you need to defend yourself as a victim.

Don't get me wrong, sometimes it is the other person who can't communicate well. And sometimes, people just act like jerks. A person might not have bad intentions toward us at all, but we hear something different. When we believe we are not at fault, we feel justified in our anger. This leaves us further and further away from what is really being communicated. What was it about the way we were communicated to that triggered an out-of-context response? Where did our misinterpretation come from?

If we've truly let go of something and put our baggage down, why is it when a person speaks in a certain tone, no matter where they might be coming from, we automatically and without thinking act inappropriately? Emotions take us to a memory that works like a reflex. It could be someone in our past who made an impression that is now hard-wired into our brain. This is called conditioning. It is how we've been trained to respond.

It may seem somewhat dehumanizing to use the word "trained," as if you've been trained like a dog. But while the word is a simplification, I find it generally to be true. If negative training is so ingrained in me, can I truly let go of what is not a part of my original energy and essence?

If you tell yourself you can't get over something, you won't. The opposite is true when you choose to say a positive affirmation. This is where I made my start; and where my positive thoughts set the stage for the many first steps of my journey.

I simply tried to be the best person I imagined I could become. Not better than anyone else, but the best version of myself—crafted by selecting the parts of me I could embrace honestly.

Conditioning has more power than people give it credit for. If you were raised on deep-fried foods, it's could be why you don't want to taste something healthy. To overcome anything in life—a lack of financial discipline, or a physical ailment—you must break away in totality from what is in the way. Refuse what is not most positive and embrace the lessons that are the catalysts for life change. Sometimes we may have to cut or limit some people from being a part of our lives.

There isn't any one path to follow to get over yourself. To learn your life's lessons and excel with love is what is most important. Love yourself. Love others. Forgive yourself. Forgive others. Stop using your ego to defend a position. Listen. React with empathy. You will always feel as another person does if you are in their shoes.

When it comes to living healthy, how many people do you know get new information that can help improve their lives, but they don't take advantage of it? Some changes are too hard to make because what is required is first admitting that your original way of doing things is wrong. It could mean questioning or doubting a lesson that came from a well-intended, trusted authority figure. It could mean that an entire belief system is wrong. If you are stuck in this place, concerned about a bruised ego in the face of necessary correction, I recommend that you stop making it all so serious. We must remove the ego from this equation to continue. Shed a different light on the whole experience. It's like going to a new restaurant that you've never been to and wanting to try everything on the menu. When you look at holistic healing as a buffet of alternative healing options instead of as a challenge to your previous belief systems, there is nothing for the ego to defend, thus making it easier to live healthy.

Intuitive energy healers and holistic practitioners have a way of seeing things that patients simply do not get from most other doctors when it comes to releasing negative conditioning. Similarly to the EFT that releases negative emotions, there are things you can do to release negative conditioning. Reiki therapy that is typically used for balancing chakras can also be used for conditioning. Acupuncture may also be employed for this purpose. You'll know that you're moving past negative conditioning by paying attention to your responses to things and the choices you make.

Once you can release the parts of your conditioning that don't serve you, you can discover what is authentically you.

This was and is not easy, but I'd like to share how I get over ME. No matter how far I get, and how much I learn, I'm always self-adjusting. Becoming self-aware is step one because you cannot fix what you are not aware of. It's how we get over ourselves and hopefully what I say can help you get over YOU.

Part Three: THE REAL YOU

After you learn and study what isn't part of your authentic self, it can be just as eye-opening and interesting to learn what is. Here are some examples on how to find out. Yes, you can study if you're a Type A, B or C personality. You can even look at your horoscope. I believe the following three people have ways toward a deeper insight of who we are.

One of many people who have been a part of my journey so far is a man named Peter Roth. Peter uses something called the "Human Design System," which involves finding your authentic personality based on the programming you were born with. His readings are remarkably accurate and clearly define what character traits are authentically yours. Everyone can act in either the best or worst versions of themselves. Energy healers may explain the difference as a high or low vibration. Are your actions of a high or low vibration? Peter Roth and his Human Design System can also explain when you are vibrating high or low based around your actions and behaviors. You may be surprised to learn that some of your negative actions and behaviors are already authentically you and not conditioning. The Human Design System shines a light on which personality traits are a high or low vibration. Also, to learn what about you is positive is also very reassuring.

My shaman, who wishes to remain nameless, also taught me something really cool. As my shaman taught me that everyone vibrates at different frequencies. My shaman has a chart that explains the difference in frequencies from person to person. The frequency number refers to how enlightened a person is. The numbers range from 100 through 800. Leonardo DaVinci vibrated at more than 700. Much of the population vibrates between 200 and 300. People who are on a spiritual path may vibrate at a higher frequency of awareness. There is also an emotional co-efficient that coincides with the frequency chart. The greatest happiness in life comes when your "enlightenment vibration" and your "emotional co-efficient vibration" are aligned. You could have a high enlightenment vibration and still have a low emotional co-efficient vibration. This means that even though you may have a certain level of spiritual awareness, you're still very emotionally reactive.

When both vibrations are aligned, the likelihood of emotional reactiveness is brought down to almost zero. Therefore, the greatest happiness is when both numbers are aligned and you're in harmony with your emotions instead of being ruled by them. It's one way to cultivate detachment like I spoke of earlier. My shaman calls it "the balancing program." There are sites on the internet where you can learn more on this topic, and specifically how to do it. The practice is to meditate on three different and specific shapes from sacred geometry for five minutes every 24 hours. The result is the ultimate in detachment. You'll have to do your own investigating if you're interested in learning this.

Another way to learn about your authentic self is a concept called "Life Energies" by Gary Null. Life Energies in my opinion focuses more on your authentic self and where it falls within the construct of a community and overall society.

When you learn about what is authentically you and operate within those findings, your life changes. So many of us get caught up in fulfilling someone else's expectation of who they feel we should be. True happiness comes to us when we break free from those obligations.

Learning who we really are can also come from our sense of spirituality. Many of us have personal reasons for desiring a connection to a higher power, and in turn, our higher selves. I don't challenge any personal reasons because different beliefs resonate with different people. My commentary comes from my own gut feeling, and wisdom gained from feeling connected to what I believe to be my higher self. As you begin to connect, you will become more attuned to your own spiritual instincts.

One of the more difficult things on this journey is learning to trust your gut. Your higher self is a consciousness and self-awareness coming from universal love. You are connected to it whether you are listening or not.

What do I refer to as "it"? "It" is the energy that powers our physical bodies—the communication between each cell in your body to work on your behalf unconditionally. This proves there is an "energy intelligence." Spirituality is awareness of and attention to the energy of the moment we are in. Spirituality allows one to obtain the feeling of physical detachment to ones' emotions, to view the world clearly in the absence of conditioned bias. For example, you can have an awareness of an emotion that has the potential to overtake you if allowed to. In that moment, option one is to detach from the emotion to act appropriately and understand your environment clearly. Option two is to react emotionally. It isn't always easy or natural to detach without effort; that's why it's a practice, and not a destination.

Spirituality is awareness through attunement to universal wisdom. As people begin a meditation routine, there always seems to be a destination involved. As a person continues the practice, eventually he or she realizes there is no destination. The state of being in the moment as an observer is the only goal. Viewing your thoughts and feelings from a place of detachment breeds clarity. The value of being unencumbered in the moment cannot be overstated.

Simple cognizance of energy without expectation allows openness to new ideas. You can go to a Buddhist meeting or any church and connect to spiritual energy. The point to any religious faith is to connect through some form of prayer. The style of prayer in any religion is a way to feel united with shared energy.

What other spiritual activities can we undertake? The most spiritual practice to engage in, is to do what you love most. When you are working on what brings you joy, you are most engaged and connected to the shared higher energy so many of us seek. It's the ultimate way to be in the moment. It's like meditating without sitting and meditating. It's why I lose track of time when I play music, cook, and put together a meal pleasing to the eye.

What activities do this for you? How can you share this with others? Can you turn it into a lifestyle that supports your life on every level? It's easy to find happiness when doing what you love and sharing it with others. When we leverage our gifts for the benefit of others we find abundance in our lives.

There are also laws within our universe.

One law is the Law of Attraction: what comes around goes around. What you put out comes back to you. What you give, you also receive. A negative thought not only can affect the intended targets, it will affect the giver as well. It's why anger can create disease. It sends a signal to the organs in the body to respond and create chemicals to make that emotion real. Now, because your body gives you the signal of anger, your mind creates more anger. That is why we must forgive others, and why we must forgive ourselves.

To achieve a balance that promotes wellness, we must also employ something that I've learned from Fotini called the Law of Manifestation. This simply means that if you have a goal, you must do only what is in line with reaching that goal and nothing that runs counter to it. At the same time, you still need to remember to not take yourself too seriously. This is the hardest, in my opinion. I believe we are always powerfully guarded by our egos. I could not do this until being healthy became such a part of me that I didn't have to think about why or justify it to anyone else. This takes time, commitment, and serious dedication. The dedication shouldn't become like a stick in your ass, either.

Your brain knows nothing because it thinks it knows everything. Yet your heart knows everything because it realizes it knows nothing. When you live through your heart it means you live with love, openness, and trust in the universe. You create your world through conscious intention and congruent action.

A big part of who we are has to do with community. As much as a person can act on a high or low vibration, so can a society. In my opinion, modern society operates on a primarily low vibration; from the powers that be, to the societal structure itself. The balance comes from groups and activists that work to create harmony within the community. Just as with an individual, harmony is the higher and healthier vibration. Modern society is organized in a way where there are winners and losers. The mentality is selfish, and the general thought is, "what's in it for me?" I don't mean this in an absolute way. Not everyone is selfish as I mentioned. I only mean that today's world is structured in a selfish way.

One problem is that most don't view the planet as a world community. Instead, everything is separated and categorized by race, religion and country, and even your hometown or village. I don't see anything wrong with having a sense of pride and love for what makes us different, or where we come from. The problem is, we use these things to feel superior. Even spiritual quests become divisive.

Deciding to learn about a spiritual path can be very alienating if the focus is on the fact that not everyone may understand you. This feeling is a little egocentric in my opinion. This is because I find that people usually tend to become very fundamentalist and absolute in their views when it comes to spirituality. Personally, I prefer an open mind when it comes to this. I find it better to go with what feels right in your heart and not from fear of death. One mistake I believe most of us make is we believe and look for things to be absolute, to be perfect. If you're vegan, you must be absolute in your belief. If you're religious, you must be absolute in your belief. Any dogma you subscribe to must be absolute. Otherwise, you're a hypocrite.

The problem with this is that energy is fluid, and too many absolutes mean energy gets stifled. We can't enjoy a spontaneous, unexpected moment of anything different because we can't betray our belief systems—especially if our identities are integrated with those beliefs. For energy to flow, we must be open and flexible. Otherwise we become stuck.

When I was younger, I was a teen with plenty of angst. Growing up in the '80s and '90s, the world seemed to be a shallow and superficial place to me. I was not interested in fitting in. In fact, I'd go out of my way to stay on the outside.

In American pop culture at that time there were punks, goths, and emo groups (among other names for teenagers) who wanted their own group but didn't want to fit in with everyone else. I had a certain perspective on the world and my place in it. While waiting to have personal relations with people I could totally connect with, I learned that it doesn't mean you can't enjoy yourself with people whose awareness is completely different.

People do not need to agree on everything to be decent, caring, and interesting to one another.

There are different levels of self and spiritual awareness, and every individual needs to find his or her own way in due time. It's easy to feel left out during this process (I certainly did); but after taking some time and training, eventually you figure out how to meet people where they are. I stopped focusing on the ways I felt different, and began to focus on the world as my community.

The downside of any journey is the judgment. People around you who are not seeking may get in competition with others who are. This attitude is the opposite of spirituality. Despite everything you will experience on your spiritual journey, never deny the uniqueness that is you or the people around you. Each of us is a light that shines differently. Love yourself to the point that you are fearless and confident; give yourself permission to be you. In your most authentic and self-actualized state, you will attract others who are like-minded. Similar energies attract.

Being a parent to a child is a great example of spiritual connection on various levels. Each person is connected. Relating to another human being comes down to meeting them where they are. While trying to connect with people who are not of your mindset, it is equally important to find your club of peers. If golf or computers or building wooden canoes is your thing, find others who share your interests.

This does not imply that you keep any company that does not respect your personal needs and limits. That is why it's important to recognize when someone is in harmony or not with you through mutual intention. It's good to offer help and love without pushing, but if you feel you are not part of their highest good or they yours, it's better to walk away. Depending on the relationship, you might not know right away where you stand with every other person. That is completely fine. It's also not our business to know where we stand with other people. Other peoples' opinions of us are not our business. I had to learn to respect the autonomy of others.

Part Four: MORE PERSONAL GROWTH

Nothing about my journey was obvious or found overnight.

I had my own trials to work through, and my own coals to walk over. Even today, I'm constantly self-correcting and learning. It's not about perfection. It was and is about being perfectly me. Love and acceptance for oneself is one of the hardest things any of us can do.

One set of coals I had to walk over was when my marriage was ending.

Even as our marriage began to fall apart, my wife was supportive. She always picked up the ball when I dropped it. At times (and especially toward the end), I took her for granted.

I have no doubt that my wife was a necessary part of my life—just as my daughter, my career path, and even my MS diagnosis was necessary.

Getting divorced is a surefire way to learn that you are not in control of anyone else's emotions and actions. Feelings of righteous entitlement can make things hard. Blame makes things hard. Not taking responsibility for my part most definitely made things hard. It seemed to be a fight the whole time, no matter what I did. All I had power over was how I chose to raise my child and how I acted. Everything I did related back to my daughter. My choices were not about me.

My ex-wife and I agreed early on to do all we could to reduce the hurt our daughter was feeling, and not punish her for her parents getting a divorce. In this very important respect, we cordially gave each other an authentic high-five outside the courtroom when divorce proceedings ended.

I searched to learn my lessons from the experience. I sought therapy. Realizing this in my session with my Shaman, my energy started to shift. In releasing anger over my divorce, this other dark monster showed up from the past. This time I could combat it once and for all. I began to cry as I released the energy. It was so intense, my body shook.

After that session with my Shaman, I became enormously depressed. I felt alone in a crowd full of people. I consulted Luanne Pennesi from Gary Null's support group on this. She explained to me that this was a perfectly normal part of growing and letting go of our former selves. It's normal to mourn the departure of everything we've come to believe is us, in exchange for something more positive and constructive. It was important for me to take time and feel it, allow it to move through me, and then finally let it go.

Learning this was essential, because it was a powerful reminder of the impermanence of everything. No storm lasts forever. If I can also look at it as a function of growth, it gives the experience a more positive outlook. So now whenever I make a shift, I expect it. It doesn't always happen, but when it does, I understand it. This makes it constructive.

A healer at a retreat explained how nothing is in vain. Every relationship is there to teach us. My anger still needed taming. Forgiveness was the key.

Even though we are all flawed, if you buy into the myth that you're bad at something, you'll cheat yourself of the chance to get good at it. True, some people have more natural ability than others, and that's OK. You must be trainable, and to be trainable is to be open. Less experience does not mean less intelligence or skill. The best athletes in the world became the best because they were trainable and listened to their coaches. The great basketball player Michael Jordan exceled for this reason. So, if there's a part of your life you feel needs improving, it's good to find a mentor.

Like my approach with physical health and healing, it was important for my financial health to find mentors. Reading books like *Rich Dad Poor Dad* by Robert Kyosaki, watching videos by Tai Lopez, and going to seminars like "The Millionaire Mind Intensive," helped rewire my brain so I could create a new state of being financially.

Talk about letting go of negative conditioning! Money is one area of life where you notice how letting go of negative conditioning can dramatically change things. What's interesting is that there are many parallels between the fundamentals of your relationship with money and your mental, emotional, spiritual and physical selves. Getting a handle on these parts can help better secure our relationships with money. One major issue for me was the inability to say no. That one problem gets so many of us in trouble, especially if you're a people pleaser. Being too impulsive in the moment and not keeping the bigger picture in your mind's eye can be a detriment.

I finally got a handle on being too impulsive with my finances, and instead trained myself to say no, set up a monthly budget, and stick to it. Finances under control, I was suddenly able to save for that rainy day.

As far as improving on the relationship with myself is concerned, rebuilding after getting out of a long relationship with another person is not easy. A sudden void creates a vacuum. I was looking to fill that void, and not in the best ways. I did not like the sense of needing anyone. Closeness to community and family was and is a great buffer, but not a replacement for another type of connection.

In trying to heal post-divorce, I spent as much time as possible getting back in balance. After everything, I'd learned that to put our personal happiness in the hands of another is a foolish game. Relearning how to be single and content was just as important as regaining my confidence.

Like with everything else, I threw myself to the wolves. I would approach random women and tell them how beautiful I thought they were, not getting tied to any expectation, just being in the moment. I would go out to social situations by myself to relieve stress and get over the awkwardness of being newly single again. My end goal was not necessarily to meet anyone, but to finally fix the relationship I had with myself.

Because I once again wanted to achieve my goals as fast as possible, I employed the help of Dr. Tian, a love coach I found online. Since the age of the internet and texting it seems men are more brazen—and not in a good way.

Dr. Tian helps men regain confidence (or find it in the first place). Learning from him was a great springboard to regaining my sense of self. When you're in a long-term, co-dependent relationship, there is a tendency to lose yourself to the other person. Having a mentor was the perfect transition back to emotional independence.

Trying to live confidently as a single parent, I know for certain that the games singles often play are not something I want any part of. I want to be happy, and therefore ended up dating someone who is also happy.

Here I am at age 40 and haven't been single since I was 24. The rules that apply when you're young are not the same when you have a child to consider. Not only do you want someone good for you, you also want someone good for your child. Then there's the whole dynamic of dividing attention. My belief is that your personal needs are just as important as your children's needs. A happy parent is a good parent. This means that the ability to be happy and single I found essential.

When you work on yourself, have your mission of self-discovery and improvement, recognize and stay in line with who you are, you can take time to know the energy of the other person. In this way partnerships can be truly equal level. We communicate to another person that we want them in our lives by our actions. Listening and understanding is step one.

As a final step in the healing process of grieving my failed marriage, I flew to Texas for a Gary Null retreat. I sought perspective and clarity; a reset button that would allow me to view life through a new set of goggles. What lessons could I take from my relationship that would bring my healing to a new level?

It was the first time in 16 years I had to focus only on myself, and me alone. Even in the peak of facing my illness I was often focused on my wife; concerned about what it was doing to her, making sure my symptoms weren't affecting her more than they had to, not letting her worry about the business when I knew it was failing. In the end, it turned out that excluding and sheltering her, even with best intentions, was my mistake. This awakening brought both regret and relief. I saw the baggage and felt its weight to put it down and feel lighter.

I knew my biggest shifts were coming toward me, because I knew at the Gary Null retreat I would get called out on my bullshit. The new me waited as I pushed the old me aside.

When I arrived, I noticed an excited energy in everyone around me. I sat quietly, open to experiencing whatever they had on deck for us to do. I understood that I could not grow if I stayed attached to the person I thought I was. It was time to clear the table and figure out who I wanted to be. I also recognized that a positive mindset would be my anchor. Attitude is where all healing and growing begins.

Not allowing ourselves to give more than we can was the first lesson at the retreat. So many of us give until we break, or until our Giving Cup is empty. This is not self-respect. Giving past our capacity is like giving someone an empty glass to drink from. If anyone needs to rest, the rule is to rest. You must learn and give yourself permission to recharge your battery.

It was my first time speaking to an audience about my experience with reversing MS. My life was at a pivotal point, like many others who were there. The energy was incredibly positive. There was a woman who suffered from MS and hadn't walked up a flight of stairs unassisted in 14 years. Every step she took didn't happen without the help of someone else lifting one leg at a time, while employing a walker. But within one week of her changing her diet and behavior, this woman was able walk up and down a set of steps with her walker, completely unassisted!

It's all about what you bring to the table each day. Being in the moment was the ultimate take-home message of the retreat.

While there, I had an opportunity with my Shaman to cut the chords of psychic attack. A psychic attack is absorbing another person's negativity toward you. Negative thoughts and feelings can penetrate your auric field and create sabotage in your life. It can block you from achieving goals and finishing projects. Psychic attacks can disrupt mental clarity like a radio signal with static interference.

On another occasion, I was doing a plumbing job at the retreat and nothing was going right. I couldn't find anything I needed to make plumbing repairs. I was trying to get parts and having zero luck with all the plumbing supply stores around. Friends were also calling me with their plumbing issues at home. Frustration was starting to take over, and I decided it was time to take a break.

When I shared these frustrations with a friend at the retreat, she empathetically suggested, "You could be the candle."

"What do you mean?" I asked.

She explained. "When you're in a dark room, you can either be part of the darkness or be a candle. You bring whatever energy you choose to any scenario. In any given moment, you can be an observer or a participant. We choose when to speak and when to listen. We can make a conscious decision to handle things as they are; not what we expect them to be. If a person is throwing anger toward you, you need not engage." Since I came to understand that it's all about what we bring to things, I've tried to bring peace as often as possible.

When I first made the decision to be a candle, I felt like a Buddha with a steak in his lap in a room full of hungry lions.

What do you bring to the table? Does your heart race when things don't go right, or when you're presented with anything negative? Yes, you can take a breath and count to 10. Yes, you can do other things to calm yourself down. Yes, you can walk away. Those are choices and solutions in the moment, and part of this lesson is taking it to the next level. When we are grounded and balanced we can do many things. We can live truly objectively by not including our emotions and ego in the conversation. Our reactions to things become appropriate without us having to work at it.

Imagine handling obstacles and confrontations from a calm, grounded, and detached perspective. What would that version of you look like? We can overcome anything with the understanding that difficult situations are all temporary. There's a solution to everything. Things may also be meant to be as they are. When you're late for work or anything important, it's for a reason. There is no need to get overzealous emotionally over things that are beyond your control.

When you need to feel empowered, consider whether you are the candle or the dark room.

Conclusion

For much of my young adult life, I was ruled by my emotions that dictated my actions. I was rarely balanced, and often angry. My search for peace was constant. One thing that I hated most in my life was conflict. Conflict is a disturbance to peace for me. I learned later that it's possible that conflicts can be resolved and lead to sustainable peace, if only I could handle the temporary discomfort of dealing with them. But back then, my choice was to sweep all my issues under the carpet. Eventually the day always comes when the dirty carpet is picked up and tossed out.

If you can imagine all the dust that it kicked up, I had a lot.

It's obvious that avoiding conflict can do harm to a relationship. I've come to learn that relationships are better off when based on mutual, shared understanding and appreciation. These attributes keep relationships in harmony. Many conflicts come from dependence, attachment and expectation.

It took the end of a 16-year relationship for me to understand this. I learned that sometimes relationships end because we don't grow otherwise. Eventually in solitude, I'd have time to reflect and learn. I realized that kindness toward me was a gift—and that it's therefore nothing short of good manners to show appreciation. I learned to not expect anything of anyone. Who am I to put that kind of responsibility on anyone else's free will? I learned to co-exist independently, emotionally and at every level in between, in harmony. I've learned to love without attachment or sense of possession.

All of this would have happened with or without the MS diagnosis. Eventually, we all reap what we have sown. And after enough of anything, there's always a tipping point. Although I believe one should give without the expectation of receiving, it is receiving that makes us want to give more. Also known as a two-way street, or the Law of Attraction. The universe acts in this way. Our bodies respond in this way. Relationships unfold in this way.

In addition to all this I learned some pretty powerful lessons in the subject of abundance. I learned that my success in business is in direct proportion to the amount of value I bring to people's lives. I stopped chasing money and began to focus on what kind of value I can bring to other people. My life is more fulfilling because I focus on the value I bring to others. I learned that if done properly, money is a natural byproduct of the value I bring to others. To me, this is happiness and fulfillment.

I broke this down to three steps.

Step one: Have an intention. Have a vision in your mind of the life you desire. Feel it in your heart as you already have it. Follow through with appropriate action. Learn as much as possible.

Step two: Understand that in life there's a flow. The only control and expectation you can have is of yourself. Swim with the current of life and not against it. Release the egoic mind's need to control everything outside of yourself.

Step three: Trust that you can make it through any challenge. You can include spiritual faith if that resonates with you. When we get anxious over a piece of bad news, we tend to act is if it determines the rest of our lives. Trust that you can make an appropriate action toward your intention.

It all goes hand in hand. When you simultaneously work on your emotional and physical health, it also becomes easier to control what habits you entertain. It's not easy, but it can be done.

I suggest to everyone reading this now to seek out your own mentors who interest you, whether it's through face-to-face counseling, reading books or watching videos. Learn every chance you get.

The most important part of your journey is investigating what resonates with *you.*

Ten years later

It's incredible to me: TEN YEARS! No wheelchair. No ramp to my house. No MS medications. No symptoms. MS Remission can last for years, but there's no telling for how long. According to my research, symptoms worsen with each relapse. So to be objective here, according to orthodox medicine I'm experiencing a really long remission.

In my opinion, I'm ten years symptom-free without meds. That's better than simply calling it remission, in my book. One doctor says I'm in a long remission. Another says I never had MS in the first place. Either way I feel truly blessed to have all the experiences I've had that led me to my greatest sense of what being healthy is.

I'm proud to share my experiences: in this book, online, and on social media. There are many levels to health and wellness. The videos I create for YouTube are geared toward individuals looking to change their lifestyle for the first time. The memes I create on FaceBook and Twitter are meant to support ideas of self-empowerment. Online I call myself The Healthy Plumber.

Speaking of self-empowerment, despite my prior difficulties with money, I've created an app to assist people in living within their means and saving money. This app is called "My Financial Freedom." This is a testament to how I've grown and implemented the knowledge I've gained. I called into Gary's radio show one night and I mentioned how I wasn't good with money. He explained to me how this was a myth and I was simply buying into it. So, if you believe that you're not good with money, don't believe it. It's a myth. Work beyond your beliefs.

The next level of health for me has been to keep growing and learning. I'm learning how to make salad sprouts. I've never been good with plants, and I'm learning to change that. I'm experimenting with different types of cleanses. Right now, I'm practicing intermittent fasting. I also keep my body in a constant state of detox. Juice and water fasting are important because it gives your body a break from constantly digesting food and allows it to focus on cleansing and repair.

I help this process along with weekly coffee enemas. Luanne taught me it's good to start a coffee enema by first cleaning your colon with warm filtered water. I incorporate lemon juice. After I clean my colon, I do the coffee enema. I lay on my right side and my back for up to 30 min. This detoxifies the liver, creates glutathione, and helps to clean the blood. A good resource to get coffee enema kits is a website called PurEnema by SeekingHealth. Through all this, I'm learning new ways to pay attention to my body and its needs.

It's through these new perspectives that I come to view my physical body in a new way. The human body is up to 60% water. The human body is also a conduit for energy and it's the movement of that energy that is our vibration. One way I found to raise my vibration is through sound. Music that plays at 432 Hertz can have a profound effect on us because how it effects the water that makes up 60% of our bodies. Eating foods that have energy to them are also vital. Playing music at 432 Hertz also helps the coffee enemas.

The balancing program of meditation has worked wonders for me. I am no longer emotionally driven, and I feel at peace and in balance. What's great about cultivating a state of being that keeps your emotions in check is you see things clearly. If a person is trying to manipulate you, you see it a mile away. I've something doesn't go as you intended it, you have perspective enough to go with the flow. You know which emotions to embrace that offer a positive outcome.

Because my ex-wife and I have a good outlook, our daughter knows peace even though it didn't work out with mom and dad. We focus on co-parenting and not on fighting. We are parents first.

She's doing great in school and enjoys dancing and drawing.

If you're reading this for the first time and struggling with symptoms, I know your pain. Do what feels right to you and don't be afraid to challenge yourself. With each failure, we learn something new. Keep your head up. Even if you cannot do any of the things mentioned, you can always start with a great attitude. Today's attitude creates tomorrow's reality.

Be patient and have faith.

Thank you so much for reading my book. I hope you found it empowering and uplifting.

No matter where you are on your journey, always know that your life is overwhelmingly blessed. Even if it doesn't seem that way. It is, and you are.

A very special thanks and shout out to all the people that helped, inspired, pushed, bluntly and constructively criticized, gave love towards this project for the past eight years. Names in alphabetical order. Beth Kallman Werner, Bob Kane, Bobby Aduna, Donna Briggs, Elizabeth Cruz, Fotini, Gary Null, Harry, Howard Robins, Jennifer May, Kristen Caldwell, Luanne Pennesi, Maryanne Christiano-Mistretta, Mathew Baker, Mom & Dad, Nicole Caldwell, Peter Roth, Richard Menashe, Skye Van Raalte-Herzog, Sophia A Ciesla, Vincent Carducci

In loving memory of
Martin Feldman and Michael Elner,

Edited by Nicole Caldwell, and Maryanne Christiano-Mistretta

Book cover design by Mathew Baker

Audio book version recorded and engineered by Vincent Carducci

Source materials for the Gary Null protocol by Luanne Pennesi with Gary Nulls permission

Matt,

    the heart that you put
into this blows me away!!!
Thank you so much for
your part in my mission!!
Couldn't have done it without you!!

        Love you bro!!

        Ken
        Coester

71131076R00083

Made in the USA
Middletown, DE
30 September 2019